the gold

of

ancient

america

by Allen Wardwell

Museum of Fine Arts, Boston

The Art Institute of Chicago

Virginia Museum

the gold of ancient america

distributed by

New York Graphic Society

Greenwich, Connecticut

Copyright 1968 by Museum of Fine Arts, Boston
The Art Institute of Chicago and Virginia Museum.
Library of Congress Catalog Card No. 68-29321

Museum of Fine Arts, Boston   December 5, 1968-January 12, 1969
The Art Institute of Chicago   February 1-March 9, 1969
Virginia Museum   March 24-April 20, 1969

Printed in the United States of America by
The Meriden Gravure Co., Meriden, Connecticut
Color plates by Philipp von Zabern, Mainz, Germany

Designed by Carl F. Zahn

contents

foreword

The gold of the Americas has held the world enthraled since the sixteenth century. But, alas, in those four hundred years man's avarice has outweighed the measure of his aesthetic response. The court of Charles V gazed in wonder and admiration at the fabulous treasure of Montezuma when it was first displayed in Spain, and Albrecht Dürer found these objects more beautiful than "the things of which miracles are made" when he saw the treasure displayed in Brussels in 1520. Yet despite the appreciation of nobleman and great artist, indeed of certain of the soldier-despoilers themselves and their clerical comrades, nearly every piece from the vast quantities of gold seized by the Conquistadores and transported to the Old World, disappeared in the melting pot long ago, an untold sacrifice to greed and power. Most of the loot of later grave robbers suffered a similar fate.

Only in our time have the golden objects of pre-Columbian America, such as the pieces that comprise this exhibition, attained a lasting value as works of art, a value that far exceeds their worth as bullion. The beholder today, like Dürer, is stirred by aesthetic delight. He is amazed at the variety of forms of the gold of the Americas, intrigued by its symbolism and function. He is aghast at the thought of its loss or deliberate destruction. These emblems of primarily stone age refinement which we cherish as gems of human skill and imagination happily remained hidden in the earth until recent times. Much of this treasure has come to light in clandestine operations in many parts of Latin America, but a considerable amount is the fruit of modern archaeological effort.

The constantly increasing interest in the art of pre-conquest America suggested that the time was ripe to present a comprehensive exhibition representative of almost all the many gold producing cultures as revealed in the finest examples obtainable as loans. In this endeavor we have been fortunate to have the services of Allen Wardwell, Curator of Primitive Art at The Art Institute of Chicago. Through his great knowledge of the subject and his acquaintance with all the principal collections of gold, he has been able to assemble an exhibition which as an endeavor to treat the subject comprehensively has not been equaled for systematic organization and expository presentation, nor for the number of masterpieces it contains.

The organization of the exhibition required the cooperation and advice of many people. Among those who supplied information and photographs of objects in their collections are Gordon F. Ekholm and Junius Bird of the American Museum of Natural History, Dudley T. Easby, Jr. of The Metropolitan Museum of Art, Elizabeth Benson of Dumbarton Oaks, Rita Campbell of the Hoover Institution on War, Revolution, and Peace. André Emmerich and John Wise have been extremely helpful in supplying photographs as well as information on the whereabouts of certain pieces in private collections. Ignacio Bernal of the Instituto Nacional de Antropologia e Historia in Mexico City was instrumental in obtaining permission for loans from the National Museum of Anthropology and from the Regional Museum of Oaxaca. Although, unfortunately, loans were not forthcoming from the countries concerned, Fernando Ortuno, Ambassador from Costa Rica, José Camacho, Minister, Colombian Embassy and Vizconde de Priego, Cultural Counselor of the Spanish Embassy were helpful with both advice and correspondence. Stanton Catlin of the Center for Inter-American Relations, New York and Landon T. Clay of Boston were extremely cooperative in trying to arrange for loans from Latin America and Spain.

The initial correspondence and typing of the catalogue was expertly handled by Marie Schwan of The Art Institute, and Patricia Alward, Editor of Publications of the Museum of Fine Arts, Boston, undertook the editorial responsibility for the catalogue.

Coordination of information at the Boston Museum was carried out by Tamsin McVickar. Installation of the exhibition was the work of Duncan Smith of the Boston Museum who revamped and adapted the display cases originally designed by William Ryan of the Virginia Museum for the exhibition of Greek gold in 1966. The catalogue was designed by Carl F. Zahn.

Particular thanks are due George Schneider of The Art Institute of Chicago who helped greatly with research and references on the catalogue entries.

Most of all we are indebted to our generous lenders — private collectors and museums in many places — whose names are listed separately. The sacrifice they have made in parting temporarily with treasured possessions has made this exhibition possible. To them, all the directors of the participating museums offer their sincere gratitude.

LESLIE CHEEK, JR.,
Director, Virginia Museum

CHARLES C. CUNNINGHAM,
Director, The Art Institute of Chicago

PERRY T. RATHBONE,
Director, Museum of Fine Arts, Boston

lenders

André Emmerich,
   New York
John H. Hauberg Collection,
   Seattle
William B. Jaffe,
   New York
Mrs. Jacob M. Kaplan,
   New York
Morton D. May,
   St. Louis
Katherine White Reswick,
   Ohio
Mrs. Bertram Smith,
   New York
Mr. and Mrs. Paul Tishman,
   New York
Benjamin Weiss,
   New York
Mr. and Mrs. Raymond Wielgus,
   Chicago
John Wise,
   New York
Suzette Morton Zurcher,
   Chicago

City Art Museum of St. Louis
Cleveland Museum of Art
Field Museum of Natural History,
   Chicago
Los Angeles County Museum of Natural History
Milwaukee Public Museum
Montreal Museum of Fine Arts
Museo Nacional de Antropologia,
   Mexico City
Museo Regional de Oaxaca
Museum of Fine Arts, Boston
Museum of the American Indian, Heye Foundation,
   New York
Peabody Museum, Harvard University,
   Cambridge
Textile Museum,
   Washington, D.C.
The Art Institute of Chicago
The Brooklyn Museum
The Museum of Primitive Art,
   New York
University Museum,
   Philadelphia
Virginia Museum,
   Richmond

introduction

To anyone familiar with the history of the Spanish conquest
of the New World, it might seem futile to attempt an exhibition such as this one. Sixteenth century accounts, as well
as those of later years, are full of descriptions of fabulous
gold pieces that will never be known to us. From Peru, for
example, such chroniclers as Cieza de Leon and Garcilaso
de la Vega write of the gold royal furniture of Atahualpa, the
Inca; the gold litter he was carried on for his first meeting
with Pizarro; his remarkable gardens which included life-
size imitations of maize, flowers and animals made of both
silver and gold; and of whole buildings and courts sheathed
in plates of gold. In addition, large vessels for drinking and
eating, cult figures and all kinds of objects of personal
adornment such as crowns, wreaths, and textile appliqués
are described. Nor were the reports from Mexico at the
time of Cortes any less impressive. Diaz del Castillo, Fray
Diego Duran and even the hardened soldier himself mar-
veled at the variety and workmanship of Mixtec gold. Again
we hear of such things as shields; vessels; the incredible
sun disk, said to have weighed 35 pounds; and innumerable
items of jewelry and costume ornament.

It is well known that the enthusiasm of the contemporary
historians was lost on the avaricious Spanish court. Nearly
every one of the thousands of pieces that were collected by
the Spaniards was melted to ingots, so that the gold could
supply capital for such ill-fated ventures as the creation of
the Armada. There are, in fact, only a handful of Mexican
gold objects collected in the sixteenth century, known to
have survived the melting pot: a group of four, wood spear
throwers with gold encrusted relief designs now in various
European museums[1] and the feather shield and headpiece
decorated with small gold plaques in the Museum für
Volkerkunde, Vienna. Undoubtedly, they owe their survival
to the small amounts of gold that were used in their construction. From Peru, nothing discovered by the conquista-
dors was spared.

Because of the autocratic nature of the two societies that
existed at the time of the conquest, the collection of Indian

1. See Saville 1925.

goldwork by the Spanish was a relatively simple affair. Both the Aztec and Inca hierarchies demanded incredible amounts of gold to be sent to the capitals as tribute, and for this reason it was readily available to the conquerors. This accounts in part for the rarity of Aztec and Inca examples today; some of the earlier styles are better represented because they were comparatively inaccessible to the Spaniards.

In ancient America gold was used only rarely for trade; rather it was looked upon as a sacred element symbolic of great power and a close alliance with the sun god. It was important as a medium for tribute payment and also sometimes was employed in the form of votive offerings, as at the Sacred Cenote at Chichen Itza, where many gold objects of Panamanian manufacture were found which had been purposely crushed before they were thrown into the water. Lastly, and of greatest significance to us, gold ornaments commonly were used in conjunction with important burials. This custom accounts for the present existence of almost every object in the exhibition; however, what has survived is only a fraction of what once existed.

Grave looting, of course, has continued to the present day, but the gold that is now thus discovered is no longer melted down, owing to the common knowledge that the objects have an even greater monetary value as art than as metal. It is probable that a certain amount of gold was reworked into new styles even in ancient times, thus accounting for an even longer history of destruction. Although many masterpieces of the goldsmith's craft have been lost and certain styles have completely disappeared (one hears, for example, of extensive amounts of gold having been made on the Antilles, but almost none is known today), it is still possible to show much of the quality of ancient American gold.

Although the working of copper was well developed among the Tarascans of Mexico and the late North Coast cultures of Peru, and there was a considerably high quality of silver-smithing, also in Peru and among the Mixtec of Mexico, gold was the only metal consistently worked throughout pre-Columbian Latin America. In comparison to the hardness of copper, and to the often impure state in which silver was found, gold was easy to work and was found in a relatively pure state. Some sixteenth century Spanish accounts refer to the existence of Indian mines, but no ancient gold mining sites have yet been discovered, although shallow shaft and open pit mines which were dug to obtain copper and silver have been found. It is probable that almost all ancient American gold was obtained from river beds by placer mining.

There is some controversy as to whether gold was worked first in Colombia or Peru, but the earliest known pieces were made about 400 B.C. by Chavin craftsmen in the North Highlands and coastal area of Peru. The evolution of gold-smithing techniques has been carefully studied and described by a number of scholars.[2] The earliest method simply involved the crude shaping of the nugget. Cold hammering and grinding were the only methods used, and the objects produced were of poor quality and have not survived in large numbers. One limitation of cold hammering was due to the phenomenon of *strain hardening*. When a piece of gold is hammered without the application of heat, it becomes increasingly brittle, and even breaks under continuing pressure.

The discovery of the annealing process solved this particular difficulty and gave the ancient goldsmith considerable freedom in working the metal. The process requires the application of a precise amount of heat to bring the gold to a soft, but not molten, state. The artist could stretch and hammer a piece of annealed gold almost indefinitely and also could decorate it with elaborate repoussé designs. Numerous sheet gold ornaments were produced by the annealing process, particularly among the cultures of Peru, Ecuador and Colombia.

The actual melting of gold and casting of it was the next significant development, and through it some of the finest

2. These findings have been summarized recently by André Emmerich, whose summary forms the basis for their brief presentation here. Emmerich 1965, pp. 158ff.

examples of ancient American gold were made. Various types of molds were used. Probably the first were simple open molds made of stone into which the molten gold was poured. Two-piece clay molds then were developed and apparently were used mostly for the casting of knives and axe blades.

Finally, the sophisticated method of lost-wax casting was discovered. This technique required the original model to be made of beeswax or resin with a low melting point into which the various details of the sculpture were modeled. The wax sculpture was covered with a coating of powdered charcoal and then with a layer of clay. When the entire mold was heated, the wax melted, poured out of a channel that had been left in the clay (thereby becoming "lost"), and the impression of the original wax sculpture remained. The mold then was filled with molten gold which took the form of the original wax model. After the gold had cooled, the mold was broken, and the gold sculpture that remained had only to be burnished and smoothed. The many small pendants from Panama and Costa Rica were made by this process.

A complex refinement of this technique was the invention of hollow core casting which allowed larger, hollow objects to be cast and also produced economy in the use of the metal itself. In this case, a rough ceramic core was modeled and then covered with wax or resin. Sculptural details were carved or added to the wax model and the entire construction was encased in clay in which various channels and air vents were left. The same process of heating the mold, allowing the melted wax to flow out and pouring the gold in was followed. When the gold piece was brought out of the mold, the core usually was broken into small pieces and disposed of. This method demanded considerable skill to keep the core, as well as the entire mold, in place while the casting was being done and was one of the major achievements of the Colombian metalworkers. Such masterpieces as the large Quimbaya figures (Cat. nos. 54 and 55) and the Sinú finials (Cat. nos. 69-71) were produced in this fashion.

A number of other techniques were used, which in conjunction with these basic methods, made possible a variety of expression and detail. Soldering with copper and silver, or copper and gold, alloys was employed to repair casting faults as well as to add sculptural details that were either too small or complex to be included in the original mold. Because an alloy of gold and copper has a relatively low melting point (about 900C.) compared to that of pure gold (1063C.) and is therefore easier to work, objects made of this compound are much more common than those of pure gold. Often after casting, a process known as *mise en couleur* was employed to bring the gold to the surface. This was achieved by rubbing the surface of a piece with acid-bearing leaves which dissolved the copper, but left the gold. It is not certain whether true plating from the mold and amalgam mercury plating were practiced, but there are some strange surviving pieces made by unknown processes, that show thin gold surfaces over cores of other metals.

Decorative techniques included incising; stamping and scratching; and inlaying with various materials such as turquoise, quartz, pyrite, amber, emerald, silver and serpentine. Repoussé and chasing were also commonly employed. Only a few methods in use today were unknown to the ancient smiths, and most of these, such as electro-plating, enameling and centrifugal casting require the use of materials and mechanical devices that did not exist in pre-Columbian America. Ecuadorean craftsmen were even able to use platinum, a difficult metal to work because of its high melting point (1773.5C.). The technique they used, known as *sintering,* involved hammering a mixture of platinum grains and gold dust on a block of charcoal, while heat was applied with the aid of a blow pipe. A malleable compound was produced although actual melting of the platinum was not achieved. The process of sintering was forgotten at the time of the conquest, not to be rediscovered until the nineteenth century.

Tools, of course, were very crude, consisting mostly of stone hammers, small copper crucibles, wood and stone rollers for smoothing wax and polishing stones and chisels.

map of major gold producing cultures and sites in pre-columbian america

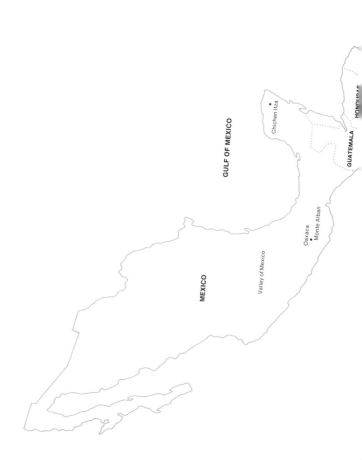

GULF OF MEXICO

MEXICO

Valley of Mexico

Oaxaca
Monte Alban

Chichen Itza

GUATEMALA

HONDURAS

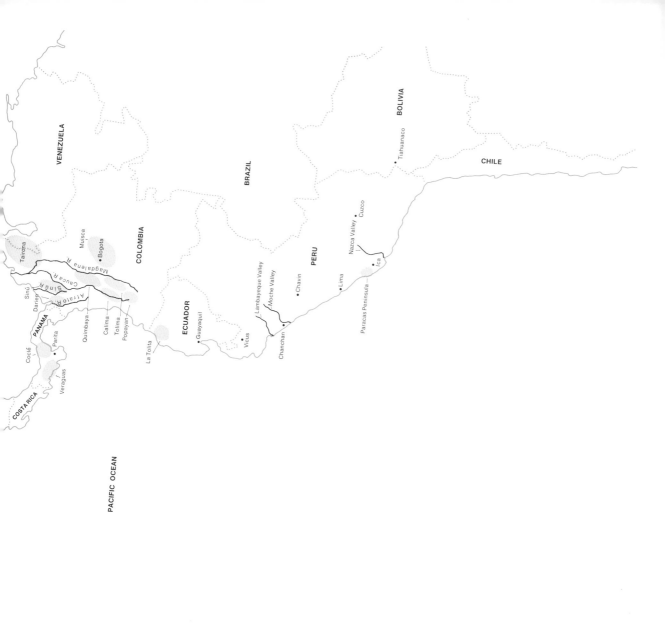

VENEZUELA

BOLIVIA

CHILE

BRAZIL

Tiahuanaco

COLOMBIA

PERU

Muisca
Bogota
Tairona
Magdalena R.

Cauca R.

Sinú
Atrato R.
Darien
Quimbaya
PANAMA
Calima
Tolima
Popayan
Cocle
Parita
Veraguas
COSTA RICA

ECUADOR
La Tolita
Guayaquil

Vicus
Chanchan
Moche Valley
Lambayeque Valley
Chavin
Lima
Nazca Valley
Cuzco
Ica
Paracas Peninsula

PACIFIC OCEAN

Some fine stone matrices over which gold was hammered or poured have survived from the Muisca culture of Colombia, but few other sophisticated implements are now known. On the whole, the primitive quality of the tools belies the fine detail and conception of the final product. To appreciate the high degree of craftsmanship of the ancient American goldsmith, one has only to consider the skill required to construct a clay mold so that molten gold would flow into all its parts. It is not surprising that the goldworkers were accorded high social positions because of their artistry. Mixtec smiths, the most talented of all ancient American metalworkers, were so highly regarded that they were not permitted to do any type of work except metalwork.

There are many different kinds of pre-Columbian gold objects, as one can see from this exhibition. More pendants and breast ornaments were made than other types of jewelry, but ear spools, nose rings, necklaces, headdress ornaments, labrets, and pins are also known. Rings, except for a few from Colombia and Panama and the elegant Mixtec examples (Cat. nos. 135 and 136), are surprisingly rare. The helmets from Colombia and Panama (Cat. no. 90) and the funerary masks from Peru (Cat. no. 22) and Colombia (Cat. no. 42) are examples of gold pieces that were made specifically for burials. Certain examples of jewelry show no signs of having been worn and must also have been made only for the dead.

Stylistically, pre-Columbian gold sculpture stands in a class by itself in comparison to gold works from other ancient cultures. We do not find the meticulous filigree and inlay that is so much a part of Greek and Etruscan jewelry. The repoussé and incising is not as fine and bold as that of Mesopotamian styles, and the exquisite cloisonné and inlay techniques of Egyptian jewelry do not find counterparts in the new world. Rather, ancient American gold owes its impact to a simple, three-dimensional treatment of form. With certain notable exceptions, particularly among the work of the Mixtec, decoration is restricted to small specific areas, and broad, unembellished surfaces form the

greater mass of each object. Repoussé ornament and other surface details emphasize but do not interfere with the overall sculptural conception.

This exhibition is not to be thought of as a catalogue of every type of gold object that was produced in pre-Columbian America, or of every style of work that has survived. The objects were chosen from the standpoint of their quality and craftsmanship. One should not look upon them as pieces of rare metal. In point of fact, their gold content is usually small, the alloys often consisting of as much as 25% copper. Rather these little sculptures should be regarded as one of the greatest technical and aesthetic achievements of the American Indian. The words of Peter Martyr, although written as long ago as 1521, come to mind as a proper and sober approach to this beautiful material. "I do not marvel at gold and precious stones, but am in a manner astonished to see the workmanship excel the substance."[3]

3. Martyr, P. (Pietro Martire d'Anghiera) De Orbe Novo Decades Octo, Alcala, 1530.

Color plate verso:

2

Pair of ear spools
Hammered, repoussé and soldered gold;
    D. 4½ inches
Lent by the Museum of the American Indian, Heye
    Foundation, New York (1972F).
Found at the Hacienda Almendral, Chongoyape,
    Chiclayo Province, Lambayeque Valley, 1928.

The design is in the form of feline faces in profile.
See note for Cat. no. 1.

References: Lothrop 1941, Pl. XVIId; Kelemen 1943,
Pl. 197a (upper right); Tello 1944, Pl. 1 (bottom
right); Bennett and Bird 1960, Fig. 24 (upper right);
Los Angeles 1964, No 164, illus.; Emmerich 1965a,
Fig. 5; Dockstader 1967, Pl. 93.

peru

In reference to Atahuallpa's ransom:

"The great heap of gold ornaments, fashioned labori-
ously by artistic Inca craftsmen, was melted down into
bars. It is reported that it took the Indian goldsmiths a
full month thus to undo their former labour, and that
nine forges were employed in the process. Of the many
other Peruvian gold ornaments that were sent intact
to Spain not a piece is known to survive; all were
melted down to bullion."
MASON, 1957.

The production of gold in Peru was probably carried on
over the longest single period of any àrea of ancient
America. The earliest pieces probably were made during
the fifth century B.C., and the metal was continuously
worked up to the Spanish conquest two thousand years
later. Although there is still some debate regarding this
question, it seems that the discovery of goldworking
occurred slightly later in Colombia.

There are many different varieties and styles of Peruvian
gold, but much of the work relies on the use of sheet gold
ornament with repoussé surface designs or bold relief
attained by hammering. Although a knowledge of casting
was acquired at an early time, it was usually only used to
make small details which were added to a hammered
piece, and complete casts are not common. Junius Bird
has recently suggested that the rarity of cast works was
caused by the lack of wax producing bees in the desert
area of the country, rather than the fact that the Peruvians
may have been inferior metalworkers.[1] Gold sculpture in
the round is also rare, appearing only sporadically during
the Mochica, Chimu and Inca periods.

1. Bird 1967, p. 22.

CHAVIN

The earliest known, worked gold pieces from Peru probably were made during the latter part of the Chavin horizon around 400-200 B.C. Almost the entire group of works to have survived comes from two caches, one near Chongoyape in the Lambayeque Valley on the North Coast, (Cat. nos. 1 and 2) and the other from the Huarmey Valley on the Central Coast (Fig. 1). Sheet gold objects including breast ornaments, ear disks, cylindrical headpieces and small plaques for application to garments are the most common forms of Chavin gold.

As would be expected, Chavin technology was not advanced, dependent as it was on such methods as hammering and repoussé application on annealed sheet gold. The relief ornament represents either stylizations of a feline deity (Cat. no. 1), one of the trademarks of the Chavin style, or simple interlocking patterns (Fig. 1). Among the most technically complex objects yet known are the pair of stirrup spout vessels now in the American Museum of Natural History (Fig. 1). Solder may have been used to keep them together, as well as careful hammering of the various parts. Simple inlay was apparently sometimes applied, but no examples have thus far been found intact.

Fig. 1

Fig. 1
Stirrup vessel and two gorgets in the Chavin style. Hammered, repoussé and (possibly) soldered gold; D. of gorgets 7½ inches, H. of vessel 10½ inches American Museum of Natural History, New York From the Huarmey Valley.
Not in exhibition.

1

Headpiece

Hammered gold; H. 9½ inches

Lent by the Museum of the American Indian, Heye
    Foundation, New York (16/1972B).

Found at the Hacienda Almendral, Chongoyape,
    Chiclayo Province, Lambayeque Valley, 1928.

This piece is part of a group of objects that includes
two other headpieces, a headband and four ear spools.
Dockstader suggests that it was "worn with a textile
band wrapped around the plain base." The design
consists of three staff gods with feline features.

References: Lothrop 1937, Fig. 93 (drawing); Lothrop
1941, Pl. XVIc and Fig. 26c; Kelemen 1943, Pl. 195b;
Tello 1944, Pl. 1 (top left); Bennett and Bird 1960,
Fig. 24; Boston Museum 1961, No. 1a,
illus.; Rowe 1962, No. 28, illus.; Los Angeles 1964, No.
163, illus.; Emmerich 1965a, Fig. 2; Dockstader 1967,
Pl. 94.

2 (see color plate p. 14)

Pair of ear spools

Hammered, repoussé and soldered gold; D. 4½ inches

Lent by the Museum of the American Indian, Heye
    Foundation, New York (16/1972F).

Found at the Hacienda Almendral, Chongoyape,
    Chiclayo Province, Lambayeque Valley, 1928.

The design is in the form of feline faces in profile. See
note for Cat. no. 1.

References: Lothrop 1941, Pl. XVIId; Kelemen 1943, Pl.
197a (upper right); Tello 1944, Pl. 1 (bottom right);
Bennett and Bird 1960, Fig. 24 (upper right); Los
Angeles 1964, No. 164, illus.; Emmerich 1965a, Fig. 5;
Dockstader 1967, Pl. 93.

1

PARACAS AND NAZCA

The Paracas culture on the South Coast, which was contemporary with the late Chavin horizon and greatly influenced by it, produced only a few gold objects, none of which are included in this exhibition. Sheet gold ornaments with simple repoussé designs are known and were attached to textiles, or were worn as forehead decorations. With only a few exceptions, the gold of Peru that was made during the Chavin and Paracas periods is two-dimensional and extremely simple in design and technique.

Similarly simple objects were made by goldworkers of the Nazca culture which followed the Paracas on the South Coast, existing from the first century to about 900 A.D. Decorative techniques were the same, basically consisting of simple repoussé patterns in geometric arrangements, some of which are in the form of animal or human faces. Emmerich uses the term "aesthetic retrogression" in regard to Nazca goldwork;[1] however, some unusually striking objects were made which owe their impact to complex cutout shapes. Among these are mouth masks, which were probably suspended from the nose (Cat. no. 3), and a group of masks or dance wands, either in the form of birds, or of human faces with serpent figures around the border (Cat. no. 4). Sheet gold forehead ornaments were also made. Nazca workmanship remained simple and was uninfluenced by the more advanced work that was being produced simultaneously in the north.

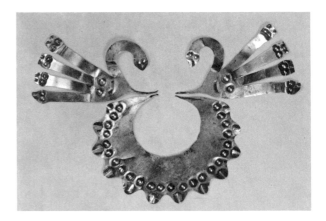

3

Mouth mask

Hammered and repoussé gold; W. 2$^{11}/_{16}$ inches

Lent by The Art Institute of Chicago, Buckingham Fund (55.2609 a-c).

Formerly in the collection of E. Gaffron, Lima.

These objects were worn in the septum of the nose and were suspended in front of the mouth. The extensions represent animal whiskers.

References: Lehmann and Doering 1924, Fig. 29; Means 1931, Fig. 51; Los Angeles 1964, Nos. 230 and 231, illus.

4

Headdress ornament or dance wand

Hammered and repoussé gold; H. 11 inches

Lent by the University Museum, Philadelphia (60-4-5).

Purchased in 1960.

1. Emmerich 1965a, p. 13.

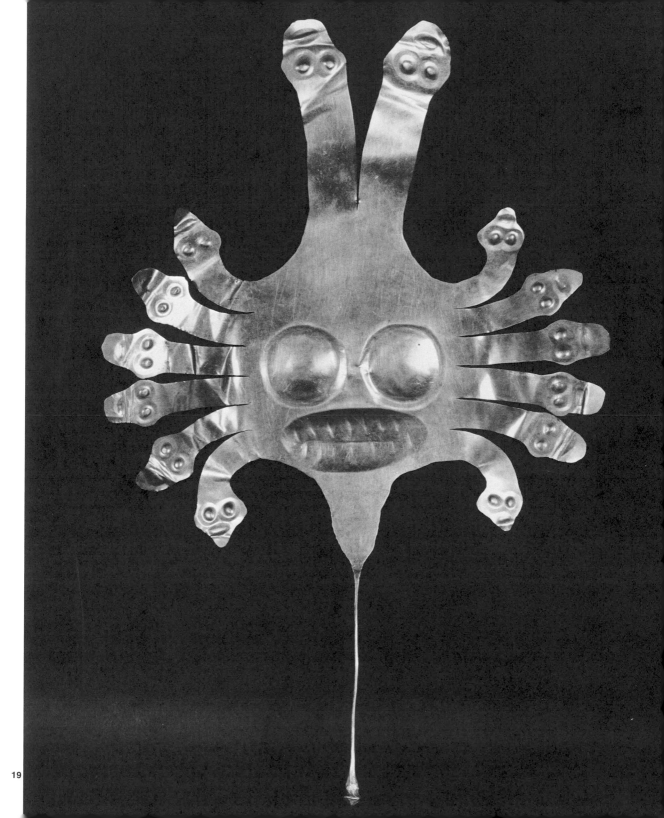

MOCHICA

The Mochica culture existed on the North Coast during the same period as the Paracas-Nazca florescence, that is, between about 400 B.C. to 900 A.D. Mochican goldwork is considerably more elaborate and advanced than anything that was being produced at the same time in the south. Although sheet gold objects with repoussé decoration were made, sculpture in-the-round was created from the earliest periods. There are a group of small animal sculptures, now thought to be from Vicus, which display one method of producing three-dimensional objects that was perfected by the Mochica (Cat. nos. 5-8). The various pieces which were to form the sculpture were hammered, perhaps over a stone matrix, bent and then joined together at the seams with solder. It was an ingenious method of working with sheet gold to produce true sculpture rather than simply, decorated, flat objects that were so common in the south at this time.

Other Mochican objects show similar concern with three-dimensional form. The spectacular headdress ornaments combine bold sculptural relief with complex animal and bird cutouts (Cat. nos. 11 and 12). Exquisite inlay was practiced particularly on some of the ear ornaments (Cat. nos. 13 and 14). Lost-wax casting was first developed by the Mochica, and copper alloys were often used. The development of the techniques of casting and alloying and the improvement of soldering allowed for the creation of many of the new and more complex styles that were to follow.

5

Jaguar ornament
Hammered and soldered gold; L. 4¼ inches
Lent by the Milwaukee Public Museum (34008).
Formerly in the collection of J. Gayoso, Lima.
Found in the vicinity of Chongoyape, Lambayeque
  Valley, 1928.

This piece is one of five known, three of which are included in this exhibition. The two others are in the Museum für Volkerkunde, Hamburg and the Mujica Gallo Museum, Lima. Lee Parsons of the Milwaukee Public Museum, who has done the preliminary research on these ornaments, believes that all were hammered over the same form. The holes in the front legs and tail were for the attachment of danglers which are still in place on the Gallo example. The use of these pieces is not known.

Reference: Boston Museum 1961, No. 4, illus.

6

Jaguar ornament
Hammered and soldered gold; L. 4 inches
Lent by the Montreal Museum of Fine Arts (60.Ad.1).
  Gift of F. Cleveland Morgan in 1960.
Originally purchased in Lima in the 1950's.
See note for Cat. no. 5.

References: Montreal Museum 1960, p. 168, illus.;
Kansas City 1962, No. 268.

7

Jaguar ornament
Hammered and soldered gold, turquoise inlay; L. 4¼
  inches
Lent by the Virginia Museum, Richmond (59-28-9).
Originally purchased in Lima in the 1950's.

The turquoise inlay is not original. See note for Cat. no. 5.

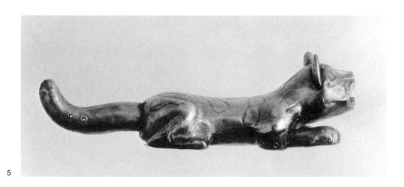

5

6

7

8
Frog ornament
Hammered and soldered gold, L. 2½ inches
Lent by Mrs. Bertram Smith, New York.
Reported to have been found near Chulucanas on the
    North Coast.

References: Los Angeles 1964, No. 174, illus.;
Emmerich 1965a, Fig. 15.

To be shown in Chicago only.

9
Nose ornament with spider figures
Cast gold; W. 4⅜ inches
Lent by The Museum of Primitive Art, New York (67.72).

An unusual example of Peruvian gold, perhaps from
the Vicus culture where such fine braiding is known
(see Washington D.C. 1965, Fig. 23).

10
Nose ring
Cast gold and silver; W. 3 inches
Lent by The Museum of Primitive Art, New York (65.62).

An ornament of similar style is in the Bliss Collection
at Dumbarton Oaks and is there attributed to the
Chimu culture from Huarmey (see Lothrop 1957, Pl.
CXXXII, No. 318). It is probably earlier and of the same
origin as Cat. no. 9.

8

10

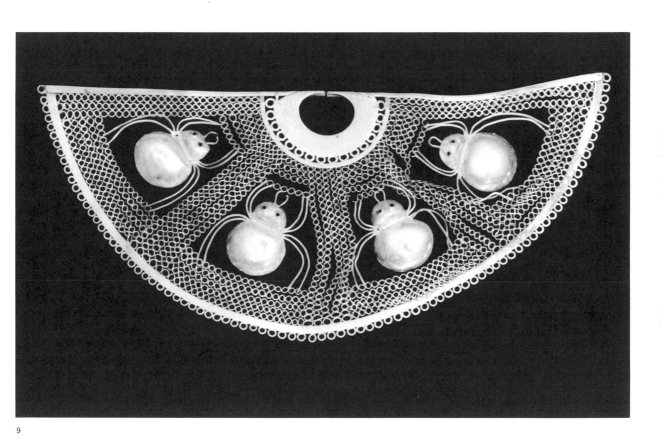

9

11
Headdress ornament
Silver with gilt, shell inlay; H. 14⅜ inches
Lent by John Wise, New York

This object is a variant of the better-known Mochica
head ornaments (see Cat. no. 12). It has been suggested that it comes from the Vicus culture, but is
probably somewhat later.

12
Head ornament with feline figure
Hammered gold; W. 10½ inches
Lent by The Museum of Primitive Art, New York
   (65.122).

This example is the mate to one in the Museo Raphael
Larco Herrera, Lima (see Emmerich 1965a, Fig. 20).

Reference: Anton and Dockstader 1968, p. 187, illus.

13

Ear ornament

Cast and hammered gold, turquoise inlay; D. 3¼ inches

Lent by The Museum of Primitive Art, New York (57.62).

A warrior is shown carrying a spear with a spear thrower. The inlays are probably not original. The mate to Cat. no. 14.

Reference: Emmerich 1965a, Fig. 24.

14

Ear ornament

Cast and hammered gold; D. 3¼ inches

Lent by the Museum of the American Indian, Heye
  Foundation, New York (16/1979).

The mate to Cat. no. 13.

13

TIAHUANACO

During the tenth and eleventh centuries the Tiahuanaco culture expanded from Bolivia into Peru and influenced cultures both in the north and south. Working of gold was not carried on to a great extent during this period. Unfortunately no examples could be included in this exhibition, but two pieces are reproduced in the catalogue to illustrate the style (Figs. 2 and 3). The beaker and the mask exemplify the simple but detailed workmanship of the best Tiahuanaco gold. Both pieces seem to have been made by the same hand and show similar relief masks and the rigid geometric ornament, based on stone relief carving, which is characteristic of the Tiahuanaco style.

Fig. 2
Beaker in the Tiahuanaco style
Hammered gold engraved with a rocker stamp; H. 4⅜
   inches
Private collection.
Not in exhibition.

Fig. 3
Mask in the Tiahuanaco style
Hammered gold engraved with a rocker stamp; H. 10½
   inches
Hoover Institution on War, Revolution and Peace,
   Stanford.
Not in exhibition.

CHIMU

The later cultures of Peru produced great quantities of gold, often at a sacrifice of quality. On the North Coast, particularly in the Lambayeque Valley during the Chimu period (c. 1200-1438), ear spools (Cat. no. 15), collars, headdress ornaments, necklaces, and ceremonial beakers (Cat. nos. 17-21) were made by the prolific goldsmiths. Many of them betray the mass production techniques of their manufacture and are comparatively tinny in appearance. Only the finest have been selected for this exhibition.

Most pieces were made from annealed sheet gold to which repoussé ornament was added. The best-known Chimu objects are the funerary masks which were affixed to mummy bundles containing the remains of prominent persons (Cat. no. 22). Large pieces of sheet gold were hammered into the form of a face; danglers, ear spools, teeth and sometimes the nose were made separately and attached with gold staples. All of these masks were originally painted and occasionally further decorated with textile or feather additions. In this form they must have been even more impressive than they are today.

Beakers were made in great numbers, mostly in the Lambayeque area; the most technologically complex are those in human head form (Cat. nos. 17 and 18). Easby has reconstructed the many steps that were required to raise such objects from a flat piece of sheet gold.[1] Continued hammering and annealing was required; facial details were molded by hammering over wooden patterns.

Also notable are ceremonial knives (Cat. no. 23), which required a great variety of techniques for their manufacture.[2] The following methods were all employed to produce each of these remarkable objects: soldering, casting, annealing, repoussé, and inlaying with turquoise. Examples other than the one shown here give evidence of gold sheathing over a wood core, the application of pigment, and even the decorative combination of alternating gold and silver areas on the blade.

1. Easby 1956, p. 403.
2. See above and Emmerich 1965a, pp. 39f.

15

15

Ear spool

Hammered repoussé and incised gold; L. 5 inches

Lent by Mr. and Mrs. Raymond Wielgus, Chicago
(58.101).

This spool is apparently the mate to one now in the
National Museum of Anthropology and Archaeology
in Lima (see Washington D.C. 1965, Fig. 84 [left]).
Although of the late Coastal Tiahuanaco period, it is
included in this section because of its close stylistic
affinity to Chimu work.

References: Museum of Primitive Art 1960, No. 104;
Los Angeles 1964, Pl. 187; Chicago Arts Club 1966,
No. 83, illus.

To be shown in Chicago only.

16

Pair of ear ornaments

Hammered and cutout gold; D. 3½ inches

Lent by The Museum of Primitive Art (57.164ab).
Possibly from the area of Trujillo.

References: Bennett 1954, Fig. 103; Museum of
Primitive Art 1958b, Pl. 50; Worcester Art Museum
1960, No. 14; Los Angeles 1964, Pl. 186; Emmerich
1965a, Fig. 33; Museum of Primitive Art 1965, Pl. 125.

16

17

18

17
Beaker
Hammered and embossed gold; H. 9½ inches
Lent by Mr. and Mrs. Paul Tishman, New York.

18
Beaker
Hammered and embossed gold; H. 10½ inches
Lent by John Wise, New York.

A figure is shown holding a shell form.

19

20

19
Beaker
Hammered and embossed gold; H. 5½ inches
Lent by John Wise, New York.

The embossed designs are in the form of shells, bird
figures and spears.

20
Beaker
Hammered and embossed gold; H. 8½ inches
Lent by John Wise, New York.

The embossed design represents birds.

21

21
Beaker
Hammered and embossed gold; H. 5⅜ inches
Lent by John Wise, New York.

The embossed designs are in the form of staffs.

22
Mask
Hammered and repoussé gold, traces of red pigment;
    W. 28¾ inches
Lent by The Museum of Primitive Art, New York
    (57.161).
From Batan Grande in the Lambayeque Valley.
Such masks were sewn to mummy bundles which
contained the remains of prominent persons. This
example is unusually large.

References: Museum of Primitive Art 1958a, Pl. 1;
Boston Museum 1961, No. 72, illus.; Emmerich 1965a,
Fig. 25; Museum of Primitive Art 1965, Pl. 124.

22

23

Ceremonial knife

Cast, hammered and repoussé gold, turquoise inlay;
  H. 13½ inches

Lent by The Art Institute of Chicago, Hertle Fund
  (63.841).

The figure on the handle is thought to represent Naym-Lap, a legendary hero who colonized the Lambayeque Valley, from which this piece originated.

References: Burlington Magazine 1964, p. 539, Pl. 74; Chicago Art Institute 1965, cover.

24

Tweezers

Hammered and soldered gold; H. 2¼ inches

Lent by the Museum of the American Indian, Heye
    Foundation, New York (15/7230).

Collected about 1925 at Chan Chan by Otto Holstein.

Reference: Dockstader 1967, Pl. 154.

25

Ornament

Cast, repoussé and hammered gold; H. 2 inches

Lent by the Museum of the American Indian, Heye
    Foundation, New York (17/8866).

Although described as an ear ornament, it is more
probable that this was used as a neck pendant.

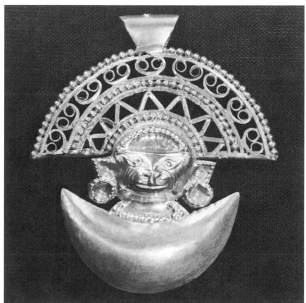

24

25

ICA

The Ica culture existed in the south contemporarily with the Chimu. From it comes a small number of gold objects, reminiscent in style of Nazca workmanship and produced for the most part by simple hammering techniques. A distinctive type of Ica gold consists of small ibis forms made of pieces of hammered gold, soldered together to form three-dimensional sculptures. Occasionally these forms appear on ear ornaments, as in the pair from The Art Institute of Chicago (Cat. no. 26). They are sometimes placed in rows and mounted together on a single piece of metal.[1]
Another form of Ica gold is represented by a fine pair of beakers with relief and unusual stipple ornament depicting birds in a corn field (Cat. no. 27).

26

26

Pair of ear ornaments (only one illus.)
Hammered and soldered gold, garnet inlay; D. 1¾ inches
Lent by The Art Institute of Chicago, Buckingham Fund (55.2594ab).
Formerly in the collection of E. Gaffron, Lima.

References: Lehmann and Doering 1924, Fig. 106b; Chicago Quarterly 1956, Vol. L, No. 1, p. 6, illus.; Kelemen 1943, Pl. 209c; Bennett 1954, Fig. 113; Chicago Art Institute 1957, p. 45, illus.; Chicago Art Institute 1965, No. 4, illus.

27

Pair of beakers
Hammered, repoussé and stippled gold; H. 2¾ inches
Lent by The Art Institute of Chicago, Buckingham Fund (55.2589ab).
Formerly in the collection of E. Gaffron, Lima.

References: Lehmann and Doering 1924, Pl. 105a; Los Angeles 1964, No. 233, illus.; Leonard 1967, p. 94, illus. (color).

1. Bird 1962, Fig. 15.

27

INCA

Technical proficiency in goldworking methods had reached a high level by the time of the Inca civilization (1438-1532). The only discovery made by Inca craftsmen was a method of inlaying metal into metal. They employed earlier techniques with great skill and made textile ornaments, cloak pins, ear spools, ceremonial vessels and breast ornaments in great numbers, many of which were subsequently destroyed by the Spaniards.

The freestanding hollow animals (Cat. nos. 30 and 31) and human figure (Cat. no. 32) are fine examples of Inca gold. These were made by carefully hammering the separate parts of the sculptures over stone or wood cores and then soldering the pieces together, a method similar to that employed by Vicus craftsmen of early Mochican times (See Cat. nos. 5-8). Some solid casts were also made (Cat. no. 29). Sixteenth century reports describe life-size hollow figures of all forms of plant and animal life. These works of incredible scale must have been masterpieces of ancient American gold. All were destroyed. The small group of miniature figures which survived must be regarded as references to the more spectacular figures which we shall never know.

One flat sheet gold ornament (Cat. no. 34), obviously not the finest example of Incan workmanship, is included in the exhibition to demonstrate the continuity of style and technique in the goldwork of Peru. The piece is important because it can be dated by the representation of a Spaniard in armor, seated on a horse, as having been made just at the time of the conquest. The artist indicated his unfamiliarity with a horse by portraying it with the cloven hooves of a llama. The feline, monkey and bird motifs, all of which had been used from the time of the Chavin horizon, are depicted with more assurance. One can see from this piece that the simplest and earliest methods of hammering, annealing and repoussé were practiced up until the beginning of the Colonial period.

28
Effigy head beaker
Hammered gold; H. 6⅝ inches
Lent by The Art Institute of Chicago, Buckingham Fund (55.2587).
Formerly in the collection of E. Gaffron, Lima.
Said to be from the South Coast.

References: Chicago Quarterly 1952, Vol. XLVI, No. 2, p. 28, illus.; Lehmann and Doering 1924, Fig. 103; Chicago Quarterly 1956, Vol. L, No. 1, p. 2, illus.; Doering 1952, Fig. 85; Bennett 1954, Fig. 100; Dockstader 1961, p. 31, illus.; Leonard 1967, p. 93, illus. (color).

29
Llama figure
Cast gold; H. 2¼ inches
Anonymous loan.
Formerly in the collection of Mrs. Claire Kauffman,
    New York.

Reference: Parke-Bernet 1968, No. 25, illus.

30

30

Llama figure
Hammered and soldered gold; H. 2⅜ inches
Lent by the City Art Museum of Saint Louis (166.54).
Gift of J. Lionberger Davis in 1954.

31

Llama figure
Hammered and soldered gold; H. 2½ inches
Lent by Katherine White Reswick, Ohio.

32

Standing female figure
Hammered and soldered gold; H. 2⅜ inches
Lent by The Museum of Primitive Art, New York
   (62.159).

Said to be from the area of Cuzco.

Reference: Museum of Primitive Art 1965, Pl. 132.

31

32

33

33

Knife

Cast gold and copper; H. 5½ inches

Lent by the University Museum, Philadelphia (SA 2826). Purchased in 1920.

The handle ornament is gold and represents an ibis. A snake is shown on the shaft of the knife. The shaft and blade are copper.

References: Kelemen 1943, Pl. 205a; Mason 1957, Fig. 41; Bird 1962, Fig. 17, illus.; Museum of Primitive Art 1964, Pl. 54.

34

Ornament, possibly an armband

Hammered and repoussé gold; L. 10 inches

Lent by The Art Institute of Chicago, Buckingham Fund (55.2608).

Formerly in the collection of E. Gaffron, Lima.

References: Chicago Art Institute 1957, p. 44, illus.; Bird 1962, Fig. 41c; Los Angeles 1964, No. 242, illus.

34

35

37
Pair of ear ornaments
Cast gold; H. ½ inch
Lent by the University Museum, Philadelphia (SA 2867).
Purchased in 1920.

Reference: Lothrop 1937, Fig. 40, p. 67.

38
Ornament in the form of a head
Hammered gold; H. ½ inch
Lent by the University Museum, Philadelphia (SA 2865).
Purchased in 1920.

Reference: Lothrop 1937, Fig. 40, p. 67.

39
Standing figure
Hammered and soldered gold; H. 1¾ inches
Lent by the Museum of the American Indian, Heye
    Foundation, New York (1/7606).
Collected by Marshall Saville in 1907 at Guayaquil.

References: Los Angeles 1964, No. 161, illus.; Dockstader 1967, Pl. 69.

INCA

40

Standing female figure

Hammered and soldered gold; H. 6 inches

Lent by the Field Museum of Natural History, Chicago (4450).

Excavated at La Plata Island, Ecuador, by George A. Dorsey, 1892.

References: Dorsey 1901, pp. 256f., Pl. XLa; Collier 1959, Fig. 88.

To be shown in Chicago only.

Color plate verso:

51
Anthropomorphic pendant
Cast gold; H. 7³/₄ inches
Lent by the Museum of the American Indian, Heye
  Foundation (5/846).
Acquired in 1919.
Said to have been found about 140 miles from the
mouth of the Rio Sinú on the east bank.

References: Kelemen 1943, Pl. 216c (center);
Basler and Brummer 1947, Pl. 129 (lower left).

colombia

The gold of Colombia presents the greatest stylistic variety of all pre-Columbian metalwork. Gold itself was comparatively plentiful; and a relatively long history of metallurgy, as well as a topography of river valleys and high mountain chains, allowed for considerable independent development. A number of separate cultures flourished in the area from the central highlands north to the Isthmus, each of which developed distinct styles and utilized a wide range of metalworking techniques.

The chronology of Colombian metalwork is far from settled; however, Perez de Barradas' division of the styles into three groups is generally accepted.[1] He places the Calima, Tolima and Darien in the early period, from about 300 B.C. to roughly 500 A.D., and the Sinu, Tairona and Muisca in the late period, from about 1000 A.D. to the time of the Conquest. He suggests that the Quimbaya style falls between the early and late periods, that is, that it came into existence shortly before the birth of Christ and lasted until about 1000 A.D. I would include the Popayan, which is not referred to in Perez de Barradas' chronological chart, in the late period.

1. Kubler 1962, p. 229 and Perez de Barradas 1966, Vol. I, p. 330.
2. Peter Furst dates the Quimbaya style from 500 A.D. to 1000 A.D. See Los Angeles 1964, p. 36.

CALIMA

It is now generally accepted that the Calima were the first metalsmiths of Colombia. The Calima region was located in the western part of Colombia at the headwaters of the Rio Cauca. The best-known works from the area are breast plates of rounded form with repoussé ornament around the rim and a bold, relief, mask form in the center (Cat. no. 41). The repoussé patterns usually are based on abstractions of the human face. Danglers in the form of nose rings and ear ornaments are often attached to the masks, sometimes obscuring much of them. These breast plates were made by hammering, annealing and stretching sheet gold. The design recalls the work of the Mochica, with which this culture is probably contemporary. Hammered burial masks (Cat. no. 42), nose rings and head decorations were also made at an early period and decorated with repoussé patterns similar to those on the breast plates.

At a later period, sometime after 100 A.D., lost-wax casting was learned, and cloak pins with beautifully sculptured figures (Cat. no. 43) and unusual pendants of figures holding masks (Cat. no. 44) were made. Detail was made separately and was soldered onto the cast forms; stone inlays were sometimes used.

41
Breast plate
Hammered, incised and repoussé gold; H. 8¾ inches
Lent by The Museum of Primitive Art, New York (57.57).

References: Museum of Primitive Art 1958b, No. 41, illus.; Kubler 1962, Pl. 116a; Los Angeles 1964, No. 121, illus.

CALIMA

"Calima smiths treated gold as if it were leather, as a pliable and impressionable substance, normally to be embossed over hard molds of stone or wood, and repoussé with dies or punches."
KUBLER, 1962.

41

42

42

Funerary mask
Cast and hammered gold; H. 6⅞ inches
Lent by John Wise, New York.

43

Cloak pin
Cast gold; H. 10¹/₁₆ inches
Lent by The Cleveland Museum of Art, Gift of the
   Hanna Fund (57.22).

Reference: Cleveland Museum 1966, p. 295, illus.
(bottom center).

43

44

44

Pendant

Cast gold; H. 2¾ inches

Lent by The Museum of Primitive Art, New York
    (57.152).

The masked figure may represent a participant in an
agricultural ceremony.

References: Museum of Primitive Art 1958b, Pl. 31;
Emmerich 1965a, Fig. 77.

TOLIMA

**The first Colombian gold casts probably were made
by Tolima craftsmen during the first century A.D.[1]
The Tolima province was located near the headwaters of the Rio Saldana, east of San Agustin. Beautiful pendants of abstract design were cast by the
lost-wax method, but only the details of the heads
were modeled in the mold and the bodies were subsequently shaped and stretched by hammering. The
forms are anthropomorphic, and the flat bodies have
four limbs (Cat. no. 45) or are sometimes winged
(Cat. nos. 46 and 47) with geometric openwork at the
sides and in the body. All of these pendants terminate
in an upturned blade form, suggesting a ceremonial
knife similar to those made in the Lambayeque
Valley of Peru (Cat. no. 23). Necklaces with miniature
figures of similar form are known.**

1. Emmerich 1965a, p. 67.

45

Anthropomorphic pendant

Cast and hammered gold; H. 9 inches

Lent by the Field Museum of Natural History, Chicago
    (6938).

Formerly in the collection of V. Restrepo who acquired
    it in 1919.

Reference: Collier 1959, No. 45, illus.

To be shown in Chicago only.

46

46

Anthropomorphic pendant
Cast and hammered gold; H. 7 inches
Lent by The Museum of Primitive Art, New York (57.46).

References: Museum of Primitive Art 1958b, Pl. 26;
Los Angeles 1964, No. 139, illus.; Museum of Primitive
Art 1965, Pl. 78; New Orleans 1968, No. 189, illus.

47

Anthropomorphic pendant
Cast and hammered gold; H. 7 inches
Lent by the University Museum, Philadelphia (SA 2754).
Purchased in 1920.

References: Farabee 1920, Fig. 51; Bennett 1954,
Fig. 180; Perez de Barradas 1958, Vol. I, p. 75, Fig. 17.

47

DARIEN

The Darien style developed in the northern part of
Colombia along the Rio Atrato at the beginning of
the Isthmus. All the gold from this area is in the form
of pendants of anthropomorphic design in varying
degrees of abstraction. The more realistic examples
(Cat. nos. 48-50) represent a standing figure with
long, flat legs, holding two staffs or rattles to the face;
strange, bell-shaped forms, which have been inter-
preted as mushrooms,[1] appear on the headdresses.
In the more abstract examples (Cat. no. 51), the figure
is barely identifiable. Simple, coffee bean shapes
form the eyes, complex spiral ornaments make up
the nose and ears; the legs are extremely flat and
stylized. The headdress ornaments and the spiral
ear forms are enlarged. Both the more realistic and
abstract types were made from lost-wax castings,
with some details, such as the mushroom ornaments
and parts of the wire decoration, being hammered or
cast separately and then soldered onto the figure.
Darien workmanship is exquisite and successfully
combines casting skill with a highly developed and
imaginative system of abstraction.

48

48
Anthropomorphic pendant
Cast gold; H. 2⅞ inches
Lent by Suzette Morton Zurcher, Chicago.

1. Emmerich 1965a, pp. 76f.

49

50

49
Anthropomorphic pendant
Cast gold; H. 3⅞ inches
Lent by The Museum of Primitive Art, New York
  (57.49).

References: Museum of Primitive Art 1958b, Pl. 1;
Kubler 1962, Pl. 117a; Emmerich 1965a, Fig. 87.

50
Anthropomorphic figure
Cast gold; H. 2¹⁵/₁₆ inches
Lent by Benjamin Weiss, New York.

This example is somewhat larger than the more common pendants in this style. As it lacks a suspension
ring, it was probably used as a votive figure rather
than a pendant.

52

51

51

Anthropomorphic pendant (see color plate, p. 56)
Cast gold; H. 7¾ inches
Lent by the Museum of the American Indian, Heye
    Foundation (5/846).
Acquired in 1919.
Said to have been found about 140 miles from the
mouth of the Rio Sinú on the east bank.

References: Kelemen 1943, Pl. 216c (center); Basler
and Brummer 1947, Pl. 129 (lower left).

52

Ornament
Cast gold; L. 3¾ inches
Lent by the Textile Museum, Washington (09.33).

The use of this piece is not certain. It is in the form of a
land snail. Although it has been traditionally attributed
to Costa Rica or the Veraguas culture of Panama, it is
in the Darien style of Colombia (see Perez de Barradas
1966, Vol. 2, Pl. 62, No. 3098, Pls. 92 and 94; Museum
of Primitive Art 1958b, Pl. 18).

Reference: Los Angeles 1964, No. 62, illus.

QUIMBAYA

Some of the finest, known examples of Colombian goldwork come from the Quimbaya culture in the central Cauca valley. The Quimbaya maintained their culture for a relatively long period and produced two distinct styles. The early pieces, which are thought to have been made during the first four or five centuries of the Christian Era, do not give any evidence of the preoccupation with mass and pure form that is such a strongly identifying feature of the castings of the later period. Most of the early work is in the form of large, sheet gold, breast plates with repoussé design and occasionally animals in relief (Cat. no. 53). Only the techniques of annealing, hammering and stretching were known to the smiths of this period.

During the later, classic period, from about 400 A.D. to 1000 A.D., remarkably large gold objects were made that required the construction of complex molds and the use of large quantities of metal. Some of the objects are in the form of human figures with naturalistic proportions and may have been used as effigies (Cat. nos. 54 and 55). Others are flasks, sometimes in the form of human figures in relief, that were used either as pendants or cinerary urns (Cat. no. 56). All of the objects from this period are highly polished and burnished. Surface detail is minimal and usually confined to small areas of decoration in the form of thin, gold threads around the wrists, knees, necks and ankles of the figures.

The treatment of gold in such completely three-dimensional terms is unique in ancient America, and the handful of large figures to have survived are among the masterworks of new world metallurgy. There are a number of works in smaller scale: figure pendants (Cat. no. 57), cylindrical nose rods (Cat. no. 58) and unusual, animal-form pendants, probably representing bats (Cat. no. 59). During the later period of their development, the Quimbaya employed the techniques of hollow core casting, repoussé, false filigree and soldering.

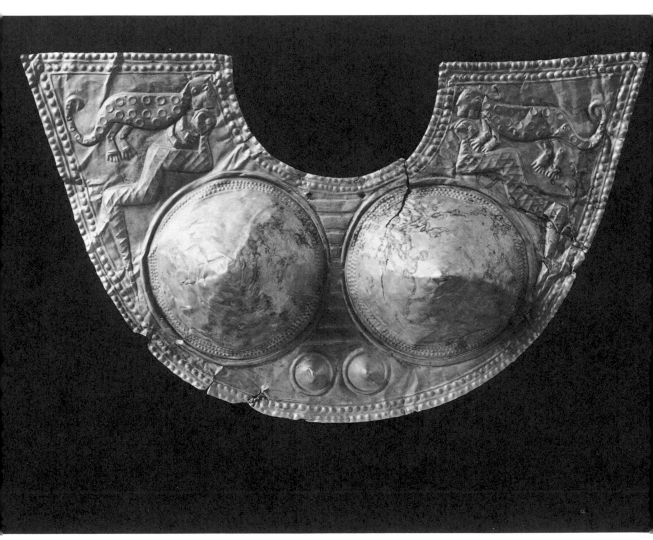

53

53

Breast plate
Hammered and repoussé gold; W. 22 inches
Lent by the University Museum, Philadelphia (SA 2703).
Purchased in 1920.
Collected in 1919 near Ayapel.

Reference: Farabee 1920, Fig. 62.

54

Seated female effigy figure
Cast gold; H. 9 inches
Lent by the University Museum, Philadelphia (SA 2751).
Purchased in 1920.

The various technical processes used to make this
piece are carefully described by Easby (1956b).

References: Farabee 1920, p. 92, Fig. 50; Lothrop 1937,
Fig. 42; Acuna 1942, p. 87, illus.; Kelemen 1943, Pl.
218d; Cleveland Museum 1946, p. 40, illus.; Bennett
1954, Fig. 171 (color); Easby 1956b, Fig. 1; Encyclo-
pedia of World Art 1959, Pl. 210; Kubler 1962, Pl. 118a;
Lothrop 1964, p. 146, illus. (color); Emmerich 1965a,
Fig. 195; Perez de Barradas 1966, Vol. I, Figs. 15, 17-20;
Man and His World 1967, No. 13, illus.

54

55 (back view)

55

Effigy figure pendant
Cast gold; H. 5⅜ inches
Lent by the Peabody Museum, Harvard University
(53971).
Purchased in 1899.

References: Kelemen 1943, Pl. 218c; Perez de Barradas 1966, Vol. I, Fig. 34 and pp. 70f (includes a detailed analysis by Dudley Easby of technique of manufacture).

56

Flask (See pp. 74, 75)
Cast gold; H. 6 inches
Lent by the Brooklyn Museum, Alfred Jenkins Fund
(35.507).
Purchased in 1935.

References: Kelemen 1943, Pl. 214a; Encyclopedia of World Art 1959, Pl. 211; Los Angeles 1964, No. 88, illus.; Perez de Barradas 1966, Vol. I, Fig. 38 and pp. 75f; Brooklyn Museum 1967, p. 233, illus.

55

57

57
Male figure pendant
Cast gold; H. 2¼ inches
Lent by The Art Institute of Chicago. Gift of Mrs. M.
    Chambers, 1923 (23.1809).

58
Nose rod
Cast gold; L. 6¾ inches
Lent by The Museum of Primitive Art, New York (63.64).

This was worn through the septum. An alligator
head decorates each end.

59
Ornament in the form of a bat
Cast gold; L. 2½ inches
Lent by the Field Museum of Natural History, Chicago
    (6931).
Formerly in the collection of V. Restrepo who acquired
    it in 1919.

To be shown in Chicago only.

58

59

77

TAIRONA

One of the least-known but finest goldworking styles of Colombia is that of the Tairona. The culture was centered in the northeastern part of the country in the Sierra Nevada de Santa Marta and seems also to have occupied part of northern Venezuela, where at least two Tairona style ornaments were found close to Lake Maracaibo.

Although there are quite a number of small gold pieces in the form of bells, nose rings and beads, castings of larger scale and more complex form are not common. The three included in this exhibition (Cat. nos. 60-62) show considerable influence of Quimbaya work in their naturalistic proportions, smoothly burnished surfaces and concern for three-dimensional form. The surface detail in the form of wire braiding is extremely fine. The example from the Los Angeles County Museum (Cat. no. 60) is further embellished by headdress ornaments of four bird heads (seen head-on and in profile) and spiral open-work which add greatly to its spectacular appearance.

Tairona craftsmen also made rattles, ear ornaments, nose rings (Cat. no. 63) and pendants in the form of birds, particularly eagles and toucans. They excelled in wax casting techniques and in the casting and application of wire ornament for surface detail. Their skill in annealing, soldering and hammering was, of course, highly developed.

60
Pendant
Cast gold; H. 5¼ inches
Lent by the Los Angeles County Museum of Natural History (67.135).

An alligator deity is represented.

Reference: Los Angeles 1964, No. 119, illus.

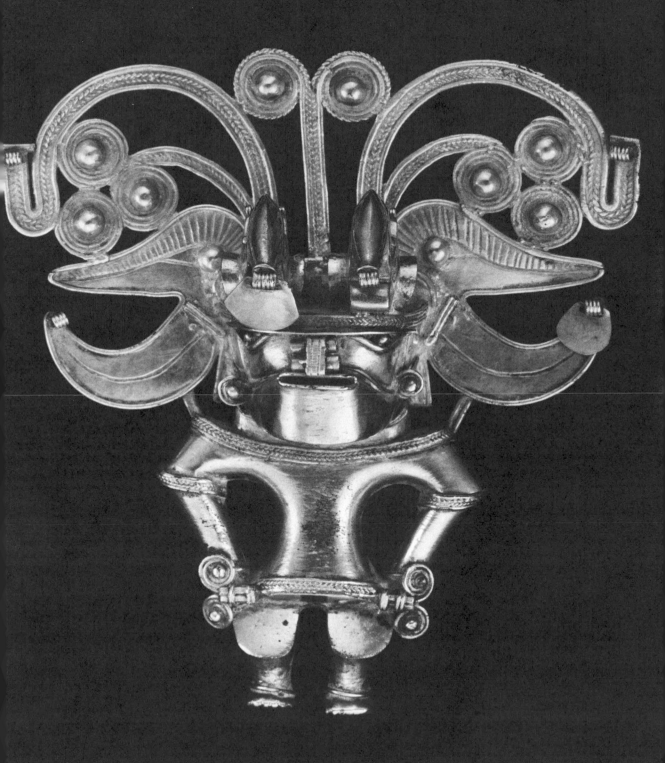

61

Male pendant figure
Cast gold; H. 3⅛ inches
Lent by The Museum of Primitive Art, New York (61.30).

Emmerich mentions the close similarity of this piece to one in the Bliss Collection (1965a, Fig. 94).

References: Emmerich 1965a, p. 81, note 10; Museum of Primitive Art 1965, No. 77, illus.

62

Seated figure
Cast gold; H. 3⁹/₁₆ inches
Lent by the Field Museum of Natural History, Chicago (153014).
Excavated at Nahuange by J. Alden Mason in 1922.

References: Mason 1936, Pl. CXLVIII and pp. 265f; Bennett 1954, Fig. 175.

To be shown in Chicago only.

63

Nose ornament
Cast gold; W. 2 inches
Lent by André Emmerich Inc., New York (B77).

62

63

SINÚ

There is a considerably larger body of work from the Sinú culture than from the Tairona. Most of it was done along the Rio Sinú, which flows into the Caribbean on the North Coast, just east of the Isthmus. The best-known pieces are elaborate, semicircular nose rings with regular geometric patterns and abstract animal or bird figures decorating the upper horizontal bar. The openwork on some examples (Cat. Nos. 64-66) is so regular and delicate that it has been theorized that net weavings were used to form the original impressions in the molds. (The same effect could have been produced by the careful placement of thin, wax strips in the mold, which is the probable method of manufacture). The nose rings with circular elements (Cat. nos. 67 and 68) display similar meticulous technique.

Sinú goldsmiths produced a number of castings of charming and imaginative animal and bird figures (Cat. nos. 69-71). The use of these objects is not certain, but they are usually referred to as baton or staff finials. They also could have been used as ornaments for litters, or other pieces of ceremonial furniture. Easby's well-known study demonstrates how these objects were cast in a single flow through the use of a complex lost-wax/clay-core technique.[1] Representations of the human figure are rare in Sinú goldwork, but occasionally appear on the smaller pendants, as on the one belonging to the Peabody Museum (Cat. no. 72) which was actually excavated at Sitio Conte in Panama.

64

Nose ring
Cast gold; L. 4 inches
Lent by the University Museum, Philadelphia (SA 2735).
Purchased in 1920.
Collected in 1919 near Ayapel.

Reference: Farabee 1920, Fig. 67 (bottom).

65

Nose ring
Cast gold; L. 3½ inches
Lent by the University Museum, Philadelphia (SA 2734).
Purchased in 1920.
Collected in 1919 near Ayapel.

Reference: Emmerich 1965a, Fig. 89 (middle).

1. The study first appeared in *Natural History Magazine* (Easby 1956, p. 406) and has been subsequently published as follows: Los Angeles 1964, p. 18 and Emmerich 1965a, Fig. 92.

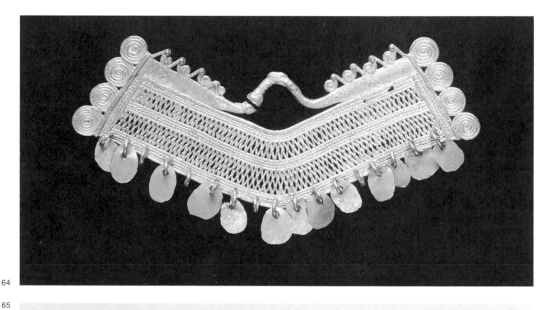

64

65

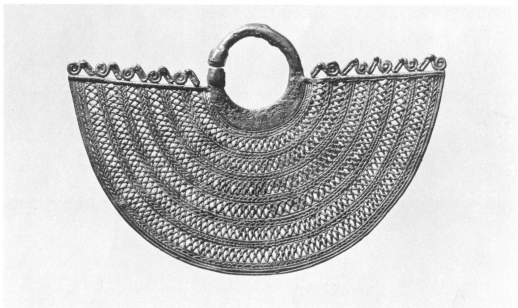

66

66

Pair of nose rings
Cast gold; L. 2⅝ inches
Lent by the Field Museum of Natural History, Chicago.
   Gift of William Wrigley, Jr. (155588).
Excavated by L. E. Melendez, June 1919, from a mound
on the Rio Nechi near Medellin.

To be shown in Chicago only.

67

Nose ring
Cast gold; L. 2½ inches
Lent by the Brooklyn Museum.

Part of the top row of ornament has broken away. Two
monkey figures can be seen at each end.

68

Nose ring
Cast gold; L. 5⅞ inches
Lent by John Wise, New York.

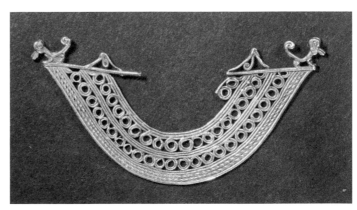

67

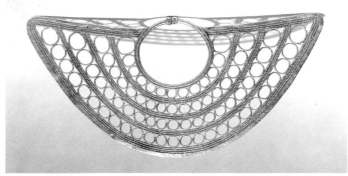

68

85

69
Bird finial
Cast gold; H. 4¾ inches
Lent by The Museum of Primitive Art, New York
    (58.281).

References: Cleveland Museum 1946, illus. (cover);
Bennett 1954, Fig. 168; Museum of Primitive Art
1958b, Pl. 5.

70
Finial with a two-headed bird figure
Cast gold; H. 4 inches
Lent by the Museum of the American Indian, Heye
    Foundation, New York. Gift of Harmon W. Hend-
    ricks, 1919 (9/2106).
Excavated in 1901 by W. B. Robbins.

References: Basler and Brummer 1947, Pl. 127 (lower
right); Dockstader 1967, Pl. 13.

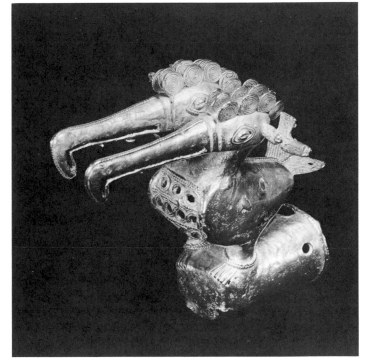

70

71

Pair of spoonbill finials
Cast gold; H. 3½-3⅞ inches
Lent by the Textile Museum, Washington (09.14 and
09.15).

72

Figure pendant
Cast gold; H. 1⅝ inches
Lent by the Peabody Museum, Harvard University
    (C11068).
Excavated at Sitio Conte, Panama in 1930 from Trench
4, grave 32.

Reference: Lothrop 1937, Fig. 151a (drawing).

72

73
Monkey pendant
Cast gold; H. 3½ inches
Lent by the Peabody Museum, Harvard University
   (C10677).
Excavated at Sitio Conte, Panama about 1929.

A similar pendant is in the Cleveland Museum (see
Cleveland Museum 1946, p. 47).

Reference: Lothrop 1937, Fig. 152.

Color plate verso:

75
Pendant
Cast gold; H. 5¼ inches
Lent by the Museum of the American Indian, Heye
    Foundation, Gift of Dr. Arthur Sackler (15/3168).
Said to be from Manizales.

References: Kelemen 1943, Pl. 217b, Dockstader
1967, Pl. 15.

POPAYAN

The rarest gold objects from Colombia are those in the Popayan style, which developed in the area near the headwaters of the Rio Cauca, not far from the border of Ecuador. The few, known pieces are bold, anthropomorphic pendants and are quite unlike any other type of ancient American gold. The extraordinary example from the Kaplan collection (Cat. no. 74) has a large, beaked nose; massive, spiral ear ornaments and oversized hands and feet. Its most striking feature, and one which it shares with two other Popayan pendants (one in the Banco de la Republica in Bogota and one in the British Museum), is its hair which is parted in the middle and extends over both shoulders in wide arcs. The Bogota and British Museum figures both stand on a thin, curved, double blade shape; the example in the exhibition does not appear to have had such a detail.

A Popayan pendant, now in the Heye Foundation (Cat. no. 75), has a human face, the body of a lizard, the hind legs of a frog and strange, wing-like forelimbs. The elaborate, openwork headdress, geometric hair and double blade shape at the bottom are reminiscent of the neighboring Tolima style. To produce these complex ornaments with such fine surface detail, Popayan smiths must have been masters of lost-wax casting techniques.

74
Male figure pendant
Cast gold; H. 4¼ inches
Lent by Mrs. Jacob M. Kaplan, New York.

The right hand of the figure was miscast and a new one was hammered and attached with three rivets.

MUISCA

The Muisca occupied an area in the central highlands near the modern city of Bogota, a situation which made them relatively isolated and allowed them to develop independently. The style of their work is unexpectedly unlike any other Colombian style. The most common Muisca objects, known as *tunjos,* are small, two-dimensional figures (Cat. nos. 76-82) which seem to have been used as votive effigies. Most are shown in standing poses and all are comparatively crude, with rough, unpolished surfaces and simplified, often grotesque, details. They were cast in one flow in molds made of wax sheets, to which wax threads were applied to form details of costume and anatomy. It would, of course, have been simpler to have soldered the gold threads in place, especially in cases where some details, such as the limbs, are separated from the flat plane of the body (see Cat. no. 79). Figures in human form are the most common; small masks, spear throwers, lizards, acquatic birds and snakes (Cat. no. 83) are known.

The Muisca also made crowns and breast ornaments. These are somewhat larger than the *tunjos* and of higher quality, and are often in the form of birds. The breast ornament included in this exhibition (Cat. no. 85) has a bold and elegant outline in the form of a bird's body which is strangely related to similar forms from the Veraguas culture in Panama, although it has not been substantiated that there was any contact between the two cultures. The surface of the piece is smoother than the *tunjos'* and the appearance of the ornament less eccentric; this apparently is due to the different method of its manufacture. A number of flat stone matrices that were molds for this type of object are known. The gold was either poured or hammered over them, and the entire process could be better controlled than in a lost-wax mold.

76

77

76

Standing figure
Cast gold; L. 3¾ inches
Lent by The Art Institute of Chicago, Gift of Mrs.
    Suzette Morton Zurcher (63.862).

77

Male figure
Cast gold; H. 3½ inches
Lent by The Art Institute of Chicago, Gift of Mrs. M. J.
    Chambers (23.1810).

Reference: Los Angeles 1964, No. 132.

78

Male figure
Cast gold; H. 4 inches
Lent by John Wise, New York

78

79

79
Seated male figure
Cast gold; H. 4¼ inches
Lent by the Field Museum of Natural History, Chicago
    (6620).
Formerly in the collection of V. Restrepo who acquired
    it in 1919.
From Songamoso.

References: Bennett 1954, Fig. 177 (center); Collier
1959, Fig. 56.

To be shown in Chicago only.

80
Standing figure
Cast gold; H. 4 inches
Lent by the Field Museum of Natural History, Chicago
    (6636).
Formerly in the collection of V. Restrepo who acquired
    it in 1919.
From Guatavita.

To be shown in Chicago only.

81
Male figure
Cast gold; H. 1⅝ inches
Lent by the Field Museum of Natural History, Chicago
    (6653).
Formerly in the collection of V. Restrepo, who pur-
    chased it in 1919.

To be shown in Chicago only.

82
Male figure
Cast gold; H. 1¼ inches
Lent by the Field Museum of Natural History, Chicago
    (6665).
Formerly in the collection of V. Restrepo who acquired
    it in 1919.

To be shown in Chicago only.

80

81

82

84

83
Snake figure
Cast gold; L. 2⅛ inches
Lent by The Art Institute of Chicago, Gift of Mrs. M. J.
    Chambers (23.1812).

84
Grotesque figure fragment
Cast gold; H. 2½ inches
Lent by John Wise, New York

An unusual example in terms of both pose and form.

85
Breast ornament
Cast and hammered gold; H. 5¼ inches
Lent by the Textile Museum, Washington (09.12).

Four bird figures are shown.

References: Kelemen 1943, Pl. 218b; Los Angeles
1964, No. 138; Anton and Dockstader 1968, p. 161,
illus. [bottom] (wrongly attributed to the Veraguas
culture of Panama).

83

85

Color plate verso:

86
Breast ornament
Hammered and embossed gold; H. 10³/₈ inches
Lent by the Peabody Museum, Harvard University
   (11036).
Excavated at Sitio Conte in 1930 from Burial C,
   grave 32.

An alligator deity is represented. This is one of the
largest examples known.

Reference: Lothrop 1937, Fig. 95.

panama

Compared to the paucity of examples from certain other areas, large numbers of gold objects from Panama have survived. These are the best-known pieces of ancient American metalwork today and were traded and used throughout widespread areas of Latin America in their own times as well. Examples have been excavated in neighboring Costa Rica, at Copan in Honduras and in Ecuador; many Panamanian pieces in the form of bells have been dredged from the Sacred Cenote at Chichen Itza where they apparently had been placed as votive offerings.

The majority of gold pieces from Panama are lost-wax castings, but other techniques such as repoussé, soldering, welding and annealing were known. In most cases the metal is a copper-gold alloy, known as *tumbaga;* the method of *mise en couleur* was employed to bring the gold to the surface of those objects with a high copper content. There are two quite distinct styles of Panamanian gold: Coclé and Veraguas.

Fig. 4
Pendant in form of a mythical animal
Cast gold; H. 2⅜ inches
Dumbarton Oaks, Washington, D.C.
From Venado Beach.
Not in exhibition.

COCLÉ

Coclé goldsmiths are thought to have begun practicing their art during the fifth century A.D. and are known to have worked until the time of the Conquest. Some of the rarest and most beautiful objects were made at Venado Beach, a site just west of the Canal. The pieces are usually pendants in the form of animals showing extremely delicate, spiral, openwork design. The pendants were made by modeling a clay core in the form of the animal. Over this core many, tiny, wax threads were laid in the intricate pattern which appears on the finished sculpture. The entire construction was then covered with a new coating of clay in which air vents and pouring vents were left. It must have been extremely difficult to make the gold flow completely through such a complex mold. Frogs are the animals most commonly represented on the pendants. The extraordinary example from Dumbarton Oaks, which unfortunately could not be included in the exhibition, is an unique representation of a mythical animal (Fig. 4). The Venado Beach site was apparently not occupied over a long period; most of the goldwork seems to have been done around the tenth century A.D.

In central Panama, the site at Sitio Conte has yielded a much larger number and greater variety of gold objects than the site at Venado Beach. However, only a few castings can match the complexity of the Venado Beach pendants. The most distinctive Sitio Conte pieces are large, hammered breast ornaments which were sewn to clothing as insignia of rank (Cat. nos. 86-89). The elaborate, animal designs which are deeply embossed on them were apparently made by pressing on a leather base with an awl. The motifs usually represent the alligator deity, but bird forms (Cat. no. 87), face designs (Cat. no. 88) and anthropomorphic figures appear as well. Burial helmets were also made with alligator deity designs (Cat. no. 90), but few have survived.

At Sitio Conte, a great number of pendants were cast in both animal and human form. Some are extremely complex, such as the famous, intricately detailed jaguar with emerald inlay from the University Mu-

seum (Cat. no. 91), or the fine, pendant, mirror frame from the Peabody Museum (Cat. no. 94) with numerous details soldered onto the cast form. Others display smooth surfaces. Alligators and alligator deities, frogs, bird forms and monkeys appear frequently. Small bells with alligator figures at the top (Cat. no. 95) were made in great quantities, apparently both for export and local use. Most of these works are hollow castings; some are inlaid with bone, shell, quartz, emerald or serpentine. Ear spools and rods, nose rings (Cat. nos. 99 and 100) and finger rings, necklaces and cuffs also were made at Sitio Conte. From this great variety of objects, it is evident that many techniques besides embossing and casting were known to the Coclé smiths. These included soldering, sheathing over wood cores and clinching.

87

Breast ornament
Hammered and embossed gold; D. 8½ inches
Lent by the University Museum, Philadelphia (40-13-2).
Excavated at Sitio Conte in 1940 by J. Alden Mason
    from Trench 2, Burial 11.

Two anthropomorphic bird deities are shown.

References: Kelemen 1943, Pl. 223b; Mason 1943, Fig. 38; Cleveland Museum 1946, p. 44, illus.

88

88

Breast ornament
Hammered and embossed gold; H. 6⅝ inches
Lent by the Peabody Museum, Harvard University
   (C11058).
Excavated at Sitio Conte in 1930 from Burial B,
   grave 32.

Reference: Lothrop 1937, Fig. 96f.

89

Breast ornament
Hammered and embossed gold; H. 4⅞ inches
Lent by André Emmerich Inc., New York (CA 429).

This ornament comes from the Parita area, to the west
of Sitio Conte on the Azuero peninsula. A similar piece,
also showing the alligator deity, is in a New York
private collection (see Emmerich 1965a, Fig. 112).

89

90

90

Burial helmet

Hammered and embossed gold; D. 8⅜ inches

Lent by the Peabody Museum, Harvard University
  (C13366).

Excavated in 1931 at Sitio Conte from Trench 1,
  grave 5.

Such helmets were placed on the heads of dead
notables at burial. The alligator deity design is shown
in various forms (see accompanying drawing).

References: Lothrop 1937, Figs. 107a, b and 108
(drawing); Kelemen 1943, Pl. 221b; Bennett 1954, Fig.
185; Los Angeles 1964, No. 11, illus. (cover); Emmerich
1965a, Fig. 113; Emmerich 1965b, p. 22; New Orleans
1968, No. 183.

90 (drawing)

91

91

Jaguar pendant

Cast gold, emerald inlay; L. 4½ inches

Lent by the University Museum, Philadelphia
    (40-13-27).

Excavated at Sitio Conte in 1940 by J. Alden Mason
    from Trench 2, Burial 11.

References: Kelemen 1943, Pl. 224d; Mason 1943,
Fig. 36; Bennett 1954, Fig. 189; Emmerich 1965a,
Fig. 114; Emmerich 1965b, p. 19, illus.

92

Pendant

Cast gold; H. 2⅝ inches

Lent by The Art Institute of Chicago, Gift of Mrs. J. Y.
    Scammon through The Antiquarian Society,
    1896 (96.115).

A male figure is shown blowing a flute.

92

93

93
Pendant
Cast gold; H. 3⁹/₁₆ inches
Lent by The Cleveland Museum of Art, Gift of Mrs.
  Benjamin P. Bole, 1946 (46.80).

Reference: Cleveland Museum 1946, p. 47 (bottom
right).

94
Pendant mirror frame
Cast gold; H. 3⅝ inches
Lent by the Peabody Museum, Harvard University
  (C13361).
Excavated at Sitio Conte in 1931 from Trench 1,
  grave 5.

Lothrop (1937, p. 105) describes the piece as a mirror
frame and suggests that the large inlay was originally
pyrite and the smaller ones of unknown material. A
being with both alligator and bat god attributes is
shown.

Reference: Lothrop 1937, frontispiece h, Figs. 47a and
71.

94

94 (back view)

95

95

Bell pendant

Cast gold; H. 1⅜ inches

Lent by the University Museum, Philadelphia
    (40-13-103).

Excavated in 1940 at Sitio Conte by J. A. Mason from
    Trench 2, Burial 11.

Two alligator figures are shown.

Reference: Mason 1943, Fig. 37.

96

Pendant whistle

Cast gold; L. 4⅝ inches

Lent by the Peabody Museum, Harvard University
    (C11057).

Excavated at Sitio Conte in 1930 from Burial C,
    grave 32.

The whistle was blown through the mouth of the
alligator (see Lothrop 1937, p. 168).

References: Lothrop 1937, frontispiece i and Fig. 154;
Dockstader 1964, Pl. 184 (top).

97

Pendant

Cast gold; L. 6⅞ inches

Lent by the Textile Museum, Washington, D.C. (09.6).

References: Kelemen 1943, Pl. 222a; Collier 1959, Pl.
44 (inside cover); Los Angeles 1964, No. 20, illus.

96

97

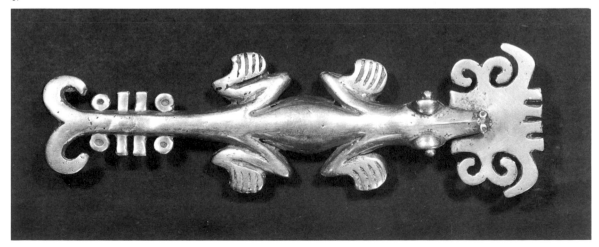

98

99

100

98
Pendant
Cast gold; H. 1 inch
Lent by the University Museum, Philadelphia
(40-13-33).
Excavated at Sitio Conte by J. A. Mason in 1940 from
Trench 2, Burial 11.

A bat is shown with wings shaped to represent alligator
deity heads in profile.

Reference: Mason 1943, Fig. 37 (upper left).

99
Nose ornament
Hammered gold; H. 2 inches
Lent by the Peabody Museum, Harvard University
(C11082).
Excavated in 1930 at Sitio Conte from Burial B,
grave 32.

An alligator is represented. Both this and Cat. no. 100
had wooden supports.

Reference: Lothrop 1937, frontispiece a, Figs. 118e
and 120b.

100
Nose ornament
Cast gold; H. 2½ inches
Lent by the Peabody Museum, Harvard University
(C10679).
Excavated at Sitio Conte in 1928.

An alligator is represented. See note for Cat. no. 99.

References: Lothrop 1937, frontispiece c, Fig. 118f;
Dockstader 1964, Pl. 184 (center).

VERAGUAS

The other major style group of Panama is usually
known as Veraguas, although the sub-styles of
Chiriqui and Diquis are ordinarily associated with
it because specific provenance is often lacking. The
Veraguas area is directly to the north of Coclé. Despite the proximity of the two areas, the goldwork of
Veraguas does not show much Coclé influence. All
pieces are lost-wax or open back castings, and the
great majority of them are animal form pendants.
Among these, the eagles (sometimes referred to as
thunderbirds or vultures) are the most renowned and
were probably made in the greatest numbers (Cat.
nos. 101-103). Their simple and boldly expressive
outlines have made them popular among collectors.
Occasionally, more than one bird appears on them
(Cat. no. 103), and often alligator heads are seen in
profile at the side of the eagle head (Cat. nos. 101,
102).

Many other animal types appear in Veraguas work.
Frogs (Cat. nos. 104, 105) were popular, apparently
as symbols of fertility; jaguars (Cat. nos. 106, 107),
well known throughout Central America as an art
motif, appear regularly; monkeys are shown play-
fully framed by their tails (Cat. no. 108); and the
alligator god, frequently painted on Panamanian
pottery, makes his appearance in gold as well.
Armadillos, turtles, and anthropomorphic figures are
also well known. The human figure is not common in
Veraguas goldwork but, when it is encountered,
evidences the same concern for smooth forms and
bold, well-balanced outlines that is found in the
animal sculptures (Cat. no. 111).

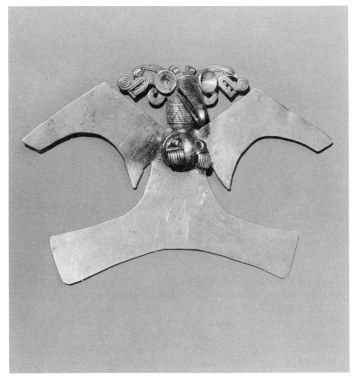

101

101

Eagle pendant
Cast gold; W. 5⅞ inches
Lent by the Museum of Primitive Art, New York
(57.143).

Two alligator deity heads in profile are seen at the
sides of the head.

References: Museum of Primitive Art 1958b, Pl. 6;
Emmerich 1965a, Fig. 137.

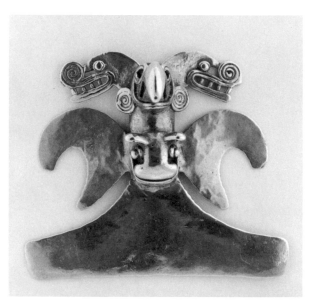

102

102
Eagle pendant
Cast gold; H. 2¾ inches
Lent by the Museum of Fine Arts, Boston, Maria
    Wharton Wales Fund (22.286). Purchased in 1922.
Formerly in the collections of John Ehrman and W.
    Wyman.

See note for Cat. no. 101.

References: Cambridge, Mass. 1940, No. 260; Kelemen
1943, Pl. 226a; Lothrop 1950, Fig. 75.

103
Double eagle pendant
Cast gold; H. 4⅜ inches
Lent by the Museum of Primitive Art, New York
    (57.140).

Reference: Museum of Primitive Art 1958b, Pl. 10.

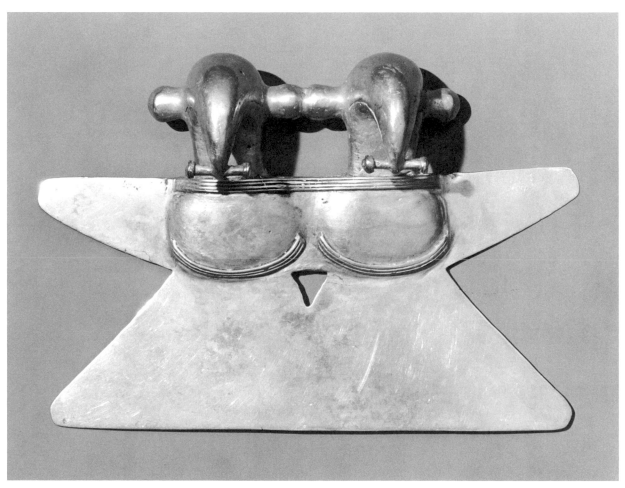

103

104

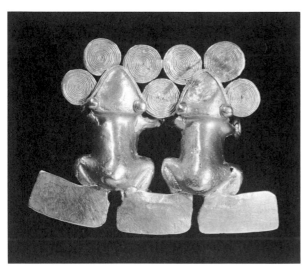

105

104

Frog pendant

Cast gold; L. 2 inches

Lent by The Art Institute of Chicago, Gift of Mrs.
　　Maurice Culberg, 1958 (58.322).

105

Double frog pendant

Cast gold; H. 2½ inches

Lent by The Cleveland Museum of Art, Gift in memory
　　of Mr. and Mrs. Henry Humphreys by their daughter,
　　Helen (46.78).

Reference: Lothrop 1950, Figs. 1e and 70c.

106

Jaguar pendant

Cast gold; L. 2⅜ inches

Lent by The Art Institute of Chicago, Gift of Mr. and
　　Mrs. Raymond Wielgus, 1965 (65.1160).

Reference: Chicago Art Institute 1957, p. 20, illus.

107

Jaguar pendant

Cast gold; L. 3 inches

Lent by the Museum of Fine Arts, Boston, Maria
　　Wharton Wales Fund (22.306). Purchased in 1922.

Formerly in the collections of J. Ehrman and W.
　　Wyman.

The jaguar is devouring a human forearm.

References: Brown 1910, p. 430, illus.; Anderson 1914,
plate facing p. 320; Cambridge, Mass. 1940, No. 259,
illus.; Lothrop 1950, Fig. 85.

108

Monkey pendant

Cast gold; H. 3 inches

Lent by the University Museum, Philadelphia (SA 2781).
　　Purchased in 1920.

Reference: Farabee 1920, Fig. 58.

106

108

107

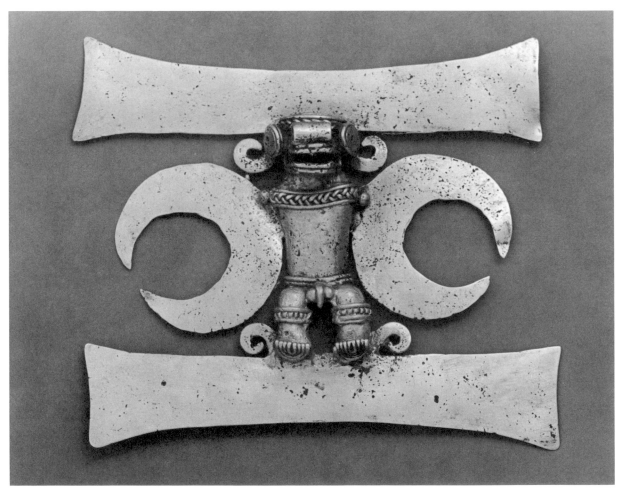

109

109
Pendant
Cast gold; H. 4¼ inches
Lent by the Museum of Primitive Art, New York
    (58.283).

An alligator deity is represented. Lothrop (1950, Fig.
110d) illustrates a similar piece which was excavated
at Zapatillo.

References: Museum of Primitive Art 1958b, Pl. 9;
Los Angeles 1964, No. 40, illus.; New Orleans 1968,
No. 184, illus.

110
Anthropomorphic pendant
Cast gold; H. 2 inches
Lent by John H. Hauberg collection, Seattle

111
Male figure pendant
Cast gold; H. 2¼ inches
Lent by The Art Institute of Chicago, Gift of Mr. and
    Mrs. Raymond Wielgus, 1966 (66.483).

110

111

Color plate verso:

120
Alligator deity pendant
Cast gold, pyrite inlay; H. 6 inches
Lent by the Museum of Primitive Art, New York
 (63.4).
From Puerto Gonzales Viquez area of Chiriqui.

References: Emmerich 1965a, Fig. 143; Museum
of Primitive Art 1965, Pl. 75.

costa rica

The goldwork of Costa Rica presents many problems of provenance and style because of its great similarity to Panamanian products. Lack of collection data usually adds to the confusion, as does the fact that there was much trading of gold ores and objects from Panama, because the metal was not plentiful in Costa Rica. Lost-wax casting of pendants was again predominant, and the major forms: birds, frogs, jaguars, alligator deities and human figures (which appear here with greater frequency than in Panama) are very close to their Veraguas counter-parts. The pieces shown here were all collected in the country, and it is reasonably certain that they were made there.

Costa Rican smiths were as skilled in casting techniques as the Panamanians, if not somewhat better. Some anthropomorphic pendants show extremely fine details (Cat. nos. 112, 113). There are a number of tiny animal pendants, such as the ones in the exhibition (Cat. nos. 114-118), which seem to have been made expressly to display their maker's skill at working in small scale. There are a few, solid, cast figures that suggest the influence of the Quimbaya style of Colombia, not only in their smooth surfaces and realistic conception, but in pose as well (Cat. no. 119).

One of the most amazing pieces from Costa Rica is the alligator deity pendant in The Museum of Primitive Art (Cat. no. 120). Its scale is impressive, and it is articulated: the head being attached to the neck by a movable link. The abdomen and eyes have pyrite inlays. The treatment of the hands, which face forward and are formed by concentric arc shapes, is typically Veraguan; as are the alligator god profile figures, which appear on the sides of the head and on both sides of the nose; and the overall naturalistic appearance of the piece.

112

112

Pendant of anthropomorphic bird deity.
Cast gold; H. 1½ inches
Lent by the Museum of Primitive Art, New York
    (57.141).

113

Male figure pendant
Cast gold; H. 4⅛ inches
Lent by the Brooklyn Museum (35.148).
Formerly in the collection of M. Kieth, New York.

References: Kelemen 1943, Pl. 231c; Vaillant 1949,
p. 81 (bottom left); Bennett 1954, Fig. 198; Spinden
1957, Pl. XXXVIIb.

114

Bird pendant
Cast gold; H. 1.2 cm.
Lent by the Brooklyn Museum (35.97).
Formerly in the collection of M. Kieth, New York.

115

Owl pendant
Cast gold; H. 1 cm.
Lent by the Brooklyn Museum (35.154).
Formerly in the collection of M. Kieth, New York.

116

Owl pendant
Cast gold; H. 1.1 cm.
Lent by the Brooklyn Museum.
Formerly in the collection of M. Kieth, New York.

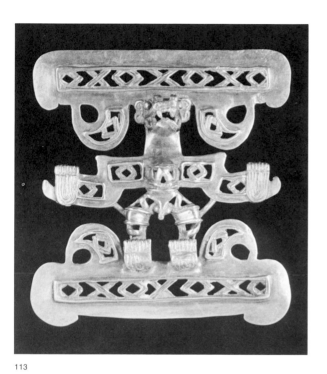

113

114

115

116

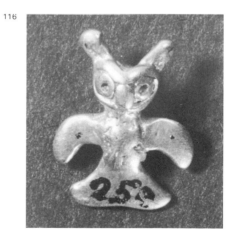

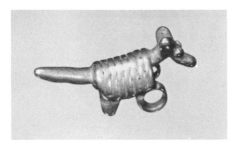

117

118

117
Armadillo pendant
Cast gold; L. 2.1 cm.
Lent by the Brooklyn Museum (35.80).
Formerly in the collection of M. Kieth, New York.

118
Bell pendant with bird figure
Cast gold; H. 2.8 cm.
Lent by the Brooklyn Museum (35.68).
Formerly in the collection of M. Kieth, New York.

119
Standing male figure
Cast gold; H. 3⅞ inches
Lent by William B. Jaffe, New York.

This figure shows considerable influence of the
Quimbaya style from Colombia and is from the area
known as Linea Vieja.

120 (see color plate, p. 126)
Alligator deity pendant
Cast gold, pyrite inlay; H. 6 inches
Lent by the Museum of Primitive Art, New York
    (63.4).
From Puerto Gonzales Viquez area of Chiriqui.

References: Emmerich 1965a, Fig. 143; Museum of
Primitive Art 1965, Pl. 75.

119

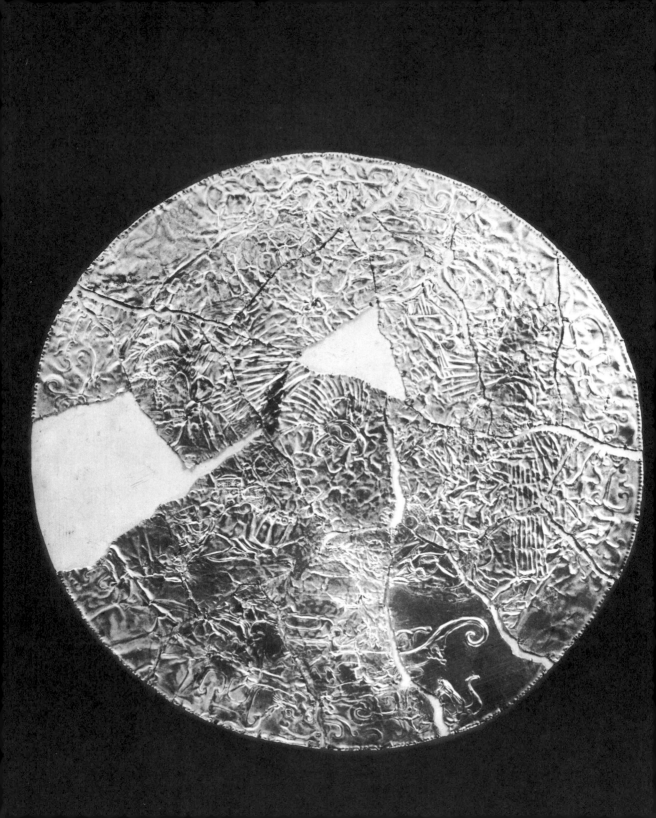

121

Disk H

Hammered and repoussé gold; D. 9 inches

Lent by the Peabody Museum, Harvard University
    (C10068).

A Toltec priest wearing an elaborate, plumed headdress is extracting the heart of a Maya warrior for
sacrifice, who is held down by a number of attendants.
The sky deity is represented above and the earth deity
below; both are included in the composition of Disks
F and B (Cat. nos. 122 and 123). This disk, which is
generally thought to be the finest, and Cat. nos. 122,
123 and 124 were dredged from the Sacred Cenote at
Chichen Itza by Edward H. Thompson between 1904
and 1907.

References: Lothrop 1952, Figs. 1 and 101, pp. 52-55;
Covarrubias 1957, Fig. 124; Los Angeles 1964, No. 5,
illus.; Emmerich 1965a, Figs. 150 and 151.

121 (drawing)

mexico

TOLTEC MAYA

**Knowledge of goldworking skills came comparatively
late to Mexico, probably only four or five centuries
before the conquest. A number of gold pieces from
the Tarascan culture are known, particularly from the
area of Jalisco on the West Coast. The objects are
hammered and annealed ornaments reminiscent of
work of the Nazca, Mochica and Chimu from Peru. A
few lost-wax castings in the form of bell pendants are
also known. Examples of Toltec Maya gold have been
found on the Yucatan Peninsula at Chichen Itza
where a number of disks with elaborate repoussé
ornament were dredged from the Sacred Cenote.
The plaques themselves, which are now in the
Peabody Museum, Harvard University and the
National Museum, Mexico City, were probably imported from Panama, as gold ores do not exist in
natural form on the Yucatan Peninsula. The ornament
on most of them portrays the conquest of Chichen
Itza by the Toltecs at the end of the tenth century.
The disks, which originally may have been mounted
on wood, are pierced for suspension and were
probably hung from the neck. They were purposely
crumpled and torn before they were thrown into the
water. It is, therefore, extremely difficult to decipher
the designs on them. (The three illustrated in the
catalogue are accompanied by drawings reconstruct-
ing the designs [Cat. nos. 121-123]). Simple annealing
and repoussé techniques were used to produce the
scenes, which are of extraordinary delicacy, recalling
the free and flowing forms of classic Maya vase
painting. Because of the close similarity it is probable
that the work was done by Maya craftsmen who were
working under Toltec domination. As the quality of
the workmanship varies, it has been suggested that
they are the work of different artists and that they
were made over a span of time. The dating of these
plaques is somewhat uncertain. Lothrop suggests
that they were made at the time of the Toltec conquest,[1] while Kubler feels that their creation
"spanned the 12th and 13th centuries."[2]**

1. Lothrop 1952, p. 111
2. Kubler 1962, p. 201

One other group of objects from the Sacred Cenote included in the exhibition are the three, sheet gold, face ornaments with bold repoussé cutouts over the eye forms, representing feathered serpents (Cat. no. 124). Again the treatment of the plumes and the flowing movements of the animal forms themselves are classic Maya in conception.

122 (drawing)

122

Disk F

Hammered and repoussé gold; D. 8⅛ inches

Lent by the Peabody Museum, Harvard University
    (C10047).

A Toltec warrior, accompanied by a spear bearer, is attacking two Maya warriors. One is seated on the ground and is attempting to extract a spear from his shoulder; the other stands and holds his spear reversed in surrender. This is the only complete disk which was not torn before being thrown into the Cenote. See Cat. no. 121.

References: Morley 1946, Fig. 57a (detail drawing); Lothrop 1952, Fig. 10f, Fig. 34 and p. 49f.

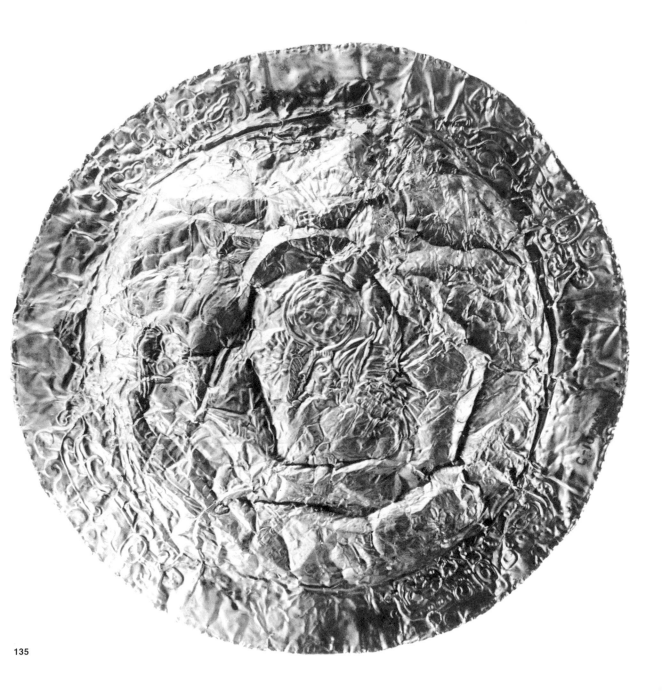

135

123

Disk B

Hammered and repoussé gold; D. 8½ inches

Lent by the Museo Nacional de Antropologia, Mexico
    City (5-1658).

Formerly in the collection of the Peabody Museum,
    Harvard University (C10065, C10072).

Two Maya prisoners are shown being interrogated by
a Toltec warrior whose attendant stands behind him.
A dish holds the head of a decapitated Maya warrior.
See Cat. no. 121.

References: Morley 1946, Fig. 57b (detail drawing);
Lothrop 1952, Fig. 10b, Fig. 30 and p. 45f.

124

Three face ornaments

Hammered and repoussé gold eye forms; H. 6¼ inches

Hammered and repoussé gold mouth form; W. 5⅞
    inches

Lent by the Peabody Museum, Harvard University
    (C7678-9).

It has been suggested that these fragments were affixed to a wooden figure which had been thrown into
the Cenote. A feathered serpent is depicted at the top
of the eye forms: the motifs on the side of the mouth
form represent abstractions of a serpent head. See
Cat. no. 121.

References: Kelemen 1943, Pl. 234b; Morley 1946,
Pl. 106c; Lothrop 1952, p. 67f and Fig. 54b; Covar-
rubias 1957, Fig. 123 (drawing); Emmerich 1965a,
Fig. 153.

123

123 (drawing)

124

MIXTEC

Soon after the introduction of simple goldworking techniques into Chichen Itza from the Isthmus, Mixtec craftsmen in the valley of Mexico near the Aztec capital of Tenochtitlan and in the state of Oaxaca around Monte Alban began to work in metal. Fine castings in copper and silver, as well as in gold, were made by these meticulous craftsmen who also learned their techniques from the Isthmus, possibly from a few teacher-artisans who were brought into the area. In a very short time the Mixtec were producing the finest gold ever to have been made in ancient America.

No monumental gold objects from any area of ancient America survived the Conquest, although it is known from contemporary accounts that they did exist. It is probable, however, that the great majority of Mixtec objects were small. Although gold deposits in Guerrero and Oaxaca were known in ancient times, the metal had to be imported into Central Mexico and was used sparingly. The examples of Mixtec gold which are known today are exquisitely detailed and were made for personal adornment.

Most of the jewelry is in the form of pendants, but labrets (Cat. nos. 126 and 127); necklaces with many small parts; rings, both to be worn on the finger tips (Cat. no. 136) and at the base of the finger (Cat. no. 135); and ear spools are known. Mixtec craftsmen employed earlier techniques with greater skill than is evident in the cultures which developed them. Lost-wax casts were made to produce relief design in false filigree (Cat. no. 135). Repoussé was meticulously applied to minute surfaces (Cat. no. 133) and bimetallic objects of gold and silver were produced, which surpassed in quality and technique their Peruvian counterparts. Gold sheathing over wooden objects (Cat. no. 125) and soldering were practiced. Some pieces were inlaid with turquoise.

Much Mixtec jewelry has a quality of motion. Pendants usually consist of more than one part, and small oval bells are often attached to them (Cat. nos. 129, 130, 132). Rings were made in similar fashion (Cat. no. 135). Other small ornaments are articulated

to give them a lifelike quality. The pendant skull with a carefully balanced lower jaw would open and close when it was worn (Cat. no. 130). Some pieces were cast in one flow of metal, while others were made in two or more molds.

The few Mixtec objects in the exhibition give ample evidence of the amazing competence of Mixtec craftsmen. Our sense of loss at the depredations of the Spanish Conquest is intensified as we become aware of the nature of the many masterpieces that were destroyed.

126
Labret with bird head
Cast gold; L. 2¼ inches
Lent by Mr. and Mrs. Raymond Wielgus, Chicago (59.145).

References: Museum of Primitive Art 1960, Pl. 9; Los Angeles 1964, No. 1, illus.; Chicago Arts Club 1966, No. 71.

To be shown in Chicago only.

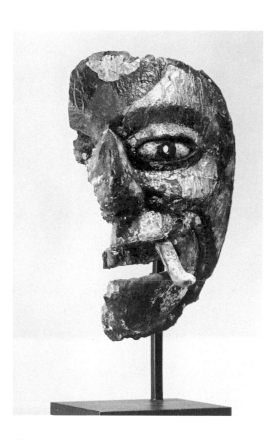 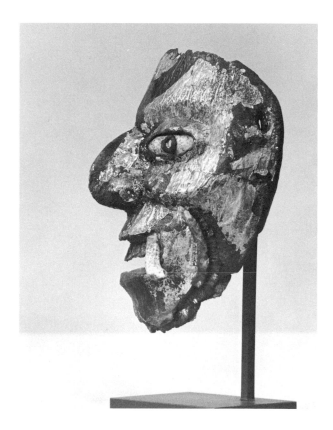

125

Mask

Wood, shell, resin, gold leaf; H. 5⅝ inches

Lent by The Art Institute of Chicago, Hertle Fund
(65.782).

This mask is said to have been found in the eastern
portion of the Yucatan Peninsula, but is believed to be
of Mixtec origin. Although not actually an example of
gold sculpture, it displays the technique of gold leaf
overlay that was practiced during the post-Classic
period in Mexico.

Reference: Chicago Calendar 1966, illus.

127

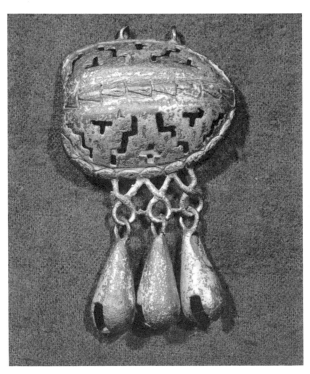

128

127

Labret with eagle head
Cast gold; L. 1½ inches
Lent by the City Art Museum of St. Louis, on loan from
    the collection of Morton D. May (68.148).

128

Pendant
Cast gold, tortoise shell; H. 3¼ inches
Lent by the Museo Nacional de Antropologia, Mexico
    City (5-1798).
From the Sacred Cenote at Chichen Itza.

Although it has been suggested that the pendant is of
Maya-Toltec origin because of its association with
Chichen Itza, it is closer in style and casting technique
to Mixtec examples. Tortoise shell is a common element in Mixtec gold objects, particularly in necklaces;
the bell pendants are also typically Mixtec.

129

Conch shell pendant
Cast gold; H. 3 inches
Lent by the Cleveland Museum of Art, John Severance
    Fund (52.86).

References: Los Angeles 1964, No. 2, illus.; Emmerich
1965a, Fig. 166; Cleveland Museum 1966, p. 292
(top center).

130

Skull pendant
Cast and soldered gold; H. 3⅜ inches
Lent by the Museo Nacional de Antropologia, Mexico
    City (7-3241).
Found at Chinantlilla, Oaxaca.

Easby (1961, pp. 38ff) has reconstructed the method of
manufacture of this piece. Two molds were used and
the lower jaw was carefully balanced and weighted so
that it would open and close with the motion of the
wearer.

References: Covarrubias 1957, Fig. 137; Easby 1961,
Fig. 1; Emmerich 1965a, Fig. 177.

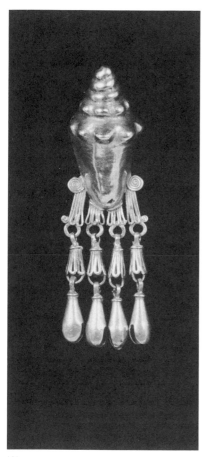

129

130

143

131

Pendant

Cast and hammered gold; H. 4⅝ inches

Lent by the Museo Nacional de Antropologia, Mexico
    City (7-2390).

Excavated by Roberto Gallegos from Tomb 2 at
Zaachila, Oaxaca in 1962.

A seated figure holding a baton is shown in the center
of a calendar disk. The body is hollow to form a bell.
The right hand base of the ornament plaque was
miscast and is attached with gold wire lacing.

References: Easby 1963, Figs. 1 and 2; Gallegos 1963,
pp. 232f, illus. (upper right); Lothrop 1964, p. 85, illus.
(color); Emmerich 1965a, Fig. 171.

131 (back view)

132

132

Pendant with eagle head
Cast gold; H. 3½ inches
Lent by the Museo Regional de Oaxaca (286).
This piece and Cat. nos. 133, 134, and 135 were excavated by Alphonso Caso in 1932 from Tomb 7 at Monte Alban, Oaxaca. The tomb was originally made and used by the Zapotecs but was used a second time for a later Mixtec burial.

From the beak of a falling eagle, said to represent the setting sun, a butterfly form (symbolic of fire) is suspended with four rows of tassel and bell attachments.

References: Caso 1932, p. 479, illus. (top); Emmerich 1965a, Fig. 162.

133

Pendant with human figure
Cast gold; H. 2⅞ inches
Lent by the Museo Regional de Oaxaca (167b).
For provenance, see Cat. no. 132.

The figure is believed to represent Xochipilli, the Aztec prince of flowers. There are four other almost identical pendants in the Tomb 7 group.

134

Pendant with anthropomorphic figure
Cast gold; H. 1⅛ inches
Lent by the Museo Regional de Oaxaca.
For provenance, see Cat. no. 132.

The flat appendages, representing legs, are similar to those found on gold animal pendants of Panama and Costa Rica. Two other examples of similar styles are in the Tomb 7 group.

133

134

135

136

135
Finger ring with eagle head
Cast gold; H. 2⅜ inches
Lent by the Museo Regional de Oaxaca (250).
For provenance, see Cat. no. 132.

References: Caso 1932, p. 479, illus. (bottom right);
Kelemen 1943, Pl. 228a; Emmerich 1965a, Fig. 164.

136
Finger ring with eagle head
Cast gold; H. ⅞ inch
Lent by the Museum of the American Indian, Heye
    Foundation (16/3417). Acquired in 1928.
Formerly in the collection of Leo Stein.

References: Lothrop 1937, Fig. 45b; Lothrop 1952,
Fig. 3b.

short title index

These references relate specifically to the text and catalogue entries and are not to be regarded as a complete bibliography of pre-Columbian gold.

Acosta 1604

Joaquin Acosta. *Compendio històrico del descubrimiento y colonizacion de la Nueva Granada en el siglo decimo sexto.* Paris, 1848.

Acuña 1942

Luis A. Acuña. *El arte de los Indios Colombianos.* Mexico City, 1942.

Anderson 1914

C. L. G. Anderson. *Old Panama and Castillo del Oro.* Boston, 1914.

Anton and Dockstader 1968

Ferdinand Anton and Frederick Dockstader. *Pre-Columbian Art and Later Indian Tribal Arts.* New York, 1968.

Basler and Brummer 1947

Adolphe Basler and Ernest Brummer. *L'Art Pre-Colombien.* Paris, 1947.

Bennett 1954

Wendell C. Bennett. *Ancient Arts of the Andes.* New York, 1954.

Bennett and Bird 1960

Wendell Bennett and Junius Bird. *Andean Culture History.* New York, 1960.

Bird 1962

Junius Bird. "Art and Life in Old Peru," *Curator,* Vol. V, No. 2. American Museum of Natural History. New York, 1962.

Bird 1967

Junius Bird, "Treasures from the Land of Gold," *Art in Virginia,* Vol. 8, Nos. 1 and 2, Richmond, 1967.

Boston Museum 1961

Twenty-five Centuries of Peruvian Art. Museum of Fine Arts. Boston, 1961.

Brooklyn Museum 1967

The Brooklyn Museum Handbook. The Brooklyn Museum. New York, 1967.

Brown 1910

C. M. Brown. "Tisingal: The Lost Mine of Panama." Bulletin of the International Bureau of the American Republics. Washington, D.C., March, 1910.

Burlington Magazine 1964

"Acquisitions of Works of Art," *Burlington Magazine,* Vol. CVI, No. 740. London, 1964.

Cambridge, Mass. 1940

An Exhibition of Pre-Columbian Art. Fogg Art Museum. Cambridge, Mass., 1940.

Caso 1932

Alfonso Caso. "Reading the Riddle of Ancient Jewels," *Natural History,* Vol. XXXII, No. 5. New York, 1932.

Chicago Art Institute 1957

Animal Sculpture in Pre-Columbian Art. Art Institute of Chicago. Chicago, 1957.

Chicago Art Institute 1965

Primitive Art in the Collections. Art Institute of Chicago. Chicago, 1965.

Chicago Calendar 1966

Allen Wardwell. "A Mixtec Mask," *Art Institute of Chicago Calendar,* Vol. LX, No. 3. Chicago, 1966.

Chicago Quarterly 1952

"Treasurers of Ancient Peruvian Art," *The Art Institute of Chicago Quarterly,* Vol. XLVI, No. 2. Chicago, 1952.

Chicago Quarterly 1956

Allan R. Sawyer. "Report on an Andean Expedition," *The Art Institute of Chicago Quarterly,* Vol. L, No. 1. Chicago, 1956.

Chicago Arts Club 1966

The Raymond and Laura Wielgus Collection. Chicago, 1966.

Cleveland Museum 1946

Art of the Americas, Picture Book, No. 2. Cleveland Museum of Art, Cleveland, 1946.

Cleveland Museum 1966

Handbook. Cleveland Museum of Art. Cleveland, 1966.

Collier 1959

Donald Collier. *Indian Art of the Americas.* Field Museum of Natural History. Chicago, 1959.

Covarrubias 1957

Miguel Covarrubias. *Indian Art of Mexico and Central America.* New York, 1957.

Dockstader 1961

Frederick J. Dockstader. "Indian Art of the Americas Before and After Columbus," *Art in America,* Vol. XLIX, No. 3. New York, 1961.

Dockstader 1964

Frederick J. Dockstader. *Indian Art in Middle America.* Greenwich, Conn., 1964.

Dockstader 1967

Frederick J. Dockstader. *Indian Art in South America.* Greenwich, Conn., 1967.

Doering 1952

Heinrich U. Doering. *The Art of Ancient Peru.* New York, 1952.

Dorsey 1901

George A. Dorsey. "Archaeological Investigations on the Island of La Plata, Ecuador," Anthropological Series II, Field Columbian Museum Publication 56. Chicago, 1901.

Easby 1956a

Dudley T. Easby. "Ancient American Goldsmiths," *Natural History,* Vol. LXV, No. 8. New York, 1956.

Easby 1956b

Dudley T. Easby. "Sahagun Reviviscit in the Gold Collection of the University Museum," University of Pennsylvania Museum Bulletin, Vol. XX, No. 3. Philadelphia, 1956.

Easby 1961

Dudley T. Easby. "Fine Metalwork in Pre-Conquest Mexico," *Pre-Columbian Art and Archaeology.* Cambridge, Mass., 1961.

Easby 1963

Dudley T. Easby. "Una nota tecnologica sobre el pectoral de Zaachila," *Sobretiro de la Revista Mexicana de Estudios Antropologicos,* Vol. IXX. Mexico, 1963.

Emmerich 1965a

André Emmerich. *Sweat of the Sun and Tears of the Moon.* Seattle, 1965.

Emmerich 1965b

André Emmerich. "Master Goldsmiths of Sitio Conte," *Natural History,* Vol. LXXIV, No. 8. New York, 1965.

Encyclopedia of World Art 1959   *Encyclopedia of World Art.* Vol. I. New York, 1959.

Farabee 1920   W. C. Farabee. "Ancient American Gold," University of Pennsylvania Museum Journal, Vol. XI, No. 3. Philadelphia, 1920.

Farabee 1921   W. C. Farabee. "A Golden Hoard from Ecuador," University of Pennsylvania Museum Journal, Vol. XII, No. 1. Philadelphia, 1921.

Gallegos 1963   Roberto Gallegos. "Zaachila: The First Season's Work," *Archaeology,* Vol. XVI, No. 4. Brattleboro, Vermont, 1963.

Kansas City 1962   "The Imagination of Primitive Man," *Bulletin of the Nelson and Atkins Museum,* Vol. IV, No. 1. Catalogue by Ralph T. Coe. Kansas City, 1962.

Kelemen 1943   Pál Kelemen. *Medieval American Art.* New York, 1943.

Kubler 1962   George Kubler. *The Art and Architecture of Ancient America.* Baltimore, 1962.

Lehmann and Doering 1924   Walter Lehmann and Heinrich U. Doering. *Kunstgeschichte des Alten Peru.* Berlin, 1924.

Leonard 1967   Jonathan Leonard. "Ancient America," *History of the World's Cultures.* New York, 1967.

Los Angeles 1964   "Gold before Columbus," *Quarterly,* Vol. II, No. 4. Catalogue by Peter Furst. Los Angeles County Museum. Los Angeles, 1964.

Lothrop 1937   Samuel K. Lothrop. *Coclé, an Archaeological Study of Central Panama.* Peabody Museum, Harvard University, Memoir, Vol. VII, Part I. Cambridge, Mass., 1937.

Lothrop 1941   Samuel K. Lothrop. "Gold Ornaments of the Chavin Style from Chongoyape, Peru," *American Antiquity,* Vol. VI, No. 3. Menasha, Wisc., 1941.

Lothrop 1950   Samuel K. Lothrop. *Archaeology of Southern Veraguas, Panama.* Peabody Museum, Harvard University, Memoir, Vol. IX, No. 3. Cambridge, Mass., 1950.

Lothrop 1952   Samuel K. Lothrop. *Metals from the Cenote of Sacrifice, Chichen Itzá, Yucatan.* Peabody Museum, Harvard University, Memoir, Vol. X, No. 2. Cambridge, Mass., 1952.

Lothrop 1957   Samuel K. Lothrop. *Pre-Columbian Art.* Robert Woods Bliss Collection. New York, 1957.

Lothrop 1964   Samuel K. Lothrop. *Treasures of Ancient America.* Geneva, 1964.

Man and His World 1967   Man and His World, Catalogue of Fine Arts Exhibition, Expo 1967. Montreal, 1967.

Mason 1936 J. Alden Mason. "Archaeology of Santa Marta, Colombia: The Tairona Culture." Field Museum of Natural History Anthropological Series, Vol. XX, No. 2. Chicago, 1936.

Mason 1943 J. Alden Mason. "The Ancient Civilizations of Middle America," University of Pennsylvania Museum Bulletin, Vol. X, Nos. 1-2. Philadelphia, 1943.

Mason 1957 J. Alden Mason. *The Ancient Civilizations of Peru*. Baltimore, 1957.

Means 1931 Philip A. Means. *Ancient Civilizations of the Andes*. New York, 1931.

Montreal Museum 1960 *Handbook of the Collections*. Montreal Museum of Fine Arts. Montreal, 1960.

Morley 1946 Sylvanus G. Morley. *The Ancient Maya*. Stanford, 1946.

Museum of Primitive Art 1958a *The Art of Ancient Peru*. The Museum of Primitive Art. New York, 1958.

Museum of Primitive Art 1958b *Pre-Columbian Gold Sculpture*. The Museum of Primitive Art. New York, 1958.

Museum of Primitive Art 1960 *The Raymond Wielgus Collection*. The Museum of Primitive Art. New York, 1960.

Museum of Primitive Art 1964 *Art of Empire, The Inca of Peru*. The Museum of Primitive Art. New York, 1964.

Museum of Primitive Art 1965 *Masterpieces in The Museum of Primitive Art, New York*. The Museum of Primitive Art. New York, 1965.

New Orleans 1968 *The Art of Ancient and Modern Latin America*. Isaac Delgado Museum of Art. New Orleans, 1968.

Parke Bernet 1968 *Pre-Columbian and North American Indian Art*. Parke Bernet Galleries, New York, Sale 2654, February 17, 1968.

Perez de Barradas 1954 José Perez de Barradas. *Orfebrería prehispánica de Colombia: Estilo Calima*. 2 vols. Madrid, 1954.

Perez de Barradas 1958 José Perez de Barradas. *Orfebrería prehispánica de Colombia: Estilos Tolima y Muisca*. 2 vols. Madrid, 1958.

Perez de Barradas 1966 José Perez de Barradas. *Orfebrería prehispánica de Colombia: Estilos Quimbaya y Otros*. 2 vols. Madrid, 1966.

Rowe 1962 John H. Rowe. *Chavin Art*. The Museum of Primitive Art. New York, 1962.

Saville 1925 Marshall Saville. *Woodcarvers Art in Ancient Mexico*. New York, 1925.

Spinden 1957 Herbert J. Spinden. *Maya Art and Civilization*. Indian Hills, Colorado, 1957.

Tello 1944   Julio C. Tello. *Sobre el descubrimiento de la cultura Chavin en el Peru*. Lima, 1944.

Vaillant 1949   George C. Vaillant. *Artists and Craftsmen in Ancient Central America*. The American Museum of Natural History. New York, 1949.

Washington, D.C. 1965   *Treasures of Peruvian Gold*. National Gallery of Art. Washington, D.C., 1965.

Worcester Art Museum 1960   *Ancient Treasures of Peru*. Worcester Art Museum. Worcester, 1960.

PHOTOGRAPH CREDITS

Unless noted below, photographs were supplied by the owners of the objects.

Art Institute of Chicago: Cat. nos. 48, 59, 66, 80, 81, 82.

Lee Boltin: Cat. no. 8.

City Art Museum of St. Louis: Cat. no. 127.

Cleveland Museum of Art: Cat. no. 31.

Dumbarton Oaks: Cat. nos. 71, 85, 97.

Dudley Easby: Cat. nos. 132-135.

André Emmerich: Fig. 2; Cat. nos. 50, 119, 131.

Peter Moore: Cat. no. 120 (color plate).

Museum of Fine Arts, Boston: Cat. no. 29.

Taylor and Dull: Cat. nos. 11, 17-21, 42, 68, 78, 84.